the Smallholder's Handbook

the Smallholder's Handbook

Keeping and caring for poultry
and livestock on a small scale

Suzie Baldwin

Photography by Rachel Warne

KYLE BOOKS

To my sister Maria, 'She Who Should Not Be Argued With', who gives a good kick up the bum when needed! Without you and your ever–suffering husband, we could never have done this. X

contents

introduction

how I got started

My childhood was a very simple one. I grew up in Devon, and my family kept a menagerie of animals, from chickens, quails, ducks and sheep to rabbits, dogs, owls, rescued hedgehogs... you name it, and I am sure that at some point we will have had one! Apart from school, my days were spent 'playing' with the animals and helping with the vegetable growing. As I recall, most of the local community produced something, whether meat, vegetables, honey, cheese or jam. My nan's gooseberries were a particular favourite of mine. Friends regularly turned up to show off and swap their produce, and evenings were spent preparing and freezing bumper crops.

When I left school, I went into nursing, and while on holiday with friends I met my husband. A very short time later, I found myself settled in an urban street in Surrey, living a very different life from the one I had known growing up. Now, with an average-sized garden and neighbours on every side, I was rather restricted. Added to this, my husband wasn't really into the 'good life' and certainly wasn't keen on the thought of the animals I hoped to have.

We had four gorgeous children, and I was determined to give them a chance to experience some of the wonderful childhood adventures I had been lucky enough to enjoy. And so, with planning and hard work, I managed to develop an urban smallholding. We had quails and chickens for meat and eggs, as well as the occasional turkey, and a lovely vegetable patch and fruit trees that soon flourished to produce an abundance of fruit.

My greatest achievement was having friends around for a meal where everything we ate had been produced in my garden. The moment was spoilt only by my telling them the name of the turkey they were eating! I learnt very quickly not to do this again. Many happy years were spent making mistakes, learning from them, and eventually getting things right.

When my children started school, I realised I wanted to do more. I was keen to share my knowledge and help people achieve the same things that I had. I ended up going into business with a man who lived locally. He was a businessman, working in London, who had 25 acres of land that he wasn't using. Although he was keen to have a taste of the 'good life', he hadn't yet done anything with his land. Between us, we set up a business called Golden Valley Poultry, raising chickens for eggs and meat, as well as keeping and selling a selection of pure breeds (which is a particular passion of mine). I managed the farm and cared for the animals, whilst he did all the

BELOW: A Pekin Cock with a Rhode Island Red Rose
Comb Bantam. OPPOSITE: Afternoon feeding time.

paperwork. Sheep came next, followed by pigs, ducks and geese, all of which proved successful endeavours. Rheas were not such a success for me, but I learnt a lot – and that's what smallholding is all about.

My passion for helping people raise productive pets led me to write my first book, *Chickens: The Essential Guide to Keeping Happy Healthy Hens*, to become a columnist for *Country Living* magazine and to produce a DVD with Joules Hudson on henkeeping, as well as holding courses and talks.

I recently bought my own smallholding, and set up my own business, Hollywater Hens, something I never thought I could afford in such an expensive and affluent area – it just goes to show that dreams can come true! Although you will never make a great deal of money through smallholding, it is possible to achieve your dreams, albeit with plenty of hard work. Having my own land makes me feel far more secure and content. I have more freedom, and no longer have to travel to lock up my animals morning and evening. If I want to, I can unlock my chickens in my pyjamas

and go back to bed with a cup of tea before starting the daily jobs a bit later – extremely welcome after a late night! But for me the biggest advantage to having my own smallholding is that it means I am on hand 24/7 to care for my charges.

In this book I want to share my knowledge of the world of smallholding. Through my own disasters and successes I have learnt a great deal, and hope that my experiences and advice will show you that, however much land you have, you can make it productive and have a truly wonderful time doing it. It will not always be easy, and a positive outlook on life is a must. You will learn to see problems (there will almost certainly be a few along the way) as 'challenges' rather than disasters; there is a solution to every problem – sometimes it might not be the answer we want, but we can't always have what we want! With the right attitude, skills and knowledge, you too can become a successful smallholder.

So whether you have an average-sized garden, one acre or six, there will be something in this book for you.

the world of smallholding

Smallholding is a very sociable way of life. Although you may spend more time with animals than people, you will quickly get to know your local fellow smallholders, who will be keen to offer and share tips and experience – and plenty of laughs! Many friends will be made and a whole new world will reveal itself to you – embrace it! Do not worry about not knowing everything; just make sure you have a good support network, whether that comes from local farmers' groups and clubs, friends, or neighbours – and, of course, a very good vet helps hugely.

Go into the world of smallholding with an open mind, ready to learn. As in many areas of life, there is no such thing as a stupid question. One of my biggest mistakes when I was younger was pretending to understand and not asking for proper explanations. So don't be scared of looking foolish – always ask questions. We all have to start somewhere. Everybody I have dealt with, from the local Trading Standards man to a very eccentric shepherd friend, have been only too happy to explain and give me invaluable advice. People who have a passion really want to share their knowledge and help others experience their wonderful way of life, so that it passes on to the next generation. If it were not for these people, some breeds would no longer even exist, so make the time to share in their knowledge.

FAR LEFT: After a visit to Tom's waterfowl farm, I'm heading home with a couple of Embden Geese. Carrying them in this way stops them flapping their wings. LEFT: You can never have too many bird cages and crates!

I could have written this book as a list of 'dos' and 'don'ts', but such is the incredible learning process of smallholding that I can assure you after a few years you would be adding to my lists. No information is set in stone and people's perceptions, expectations and levels of commitment are all variables. Smallholders often have very different reasons for keeping animals – for example, some don't want to raise their animals for food, while for others this is their main purpose (my mad neighbour Gill always says, 'If you cannot eat it – do not keep it.').

Take your time when starting out – building up your livestock gradually is extremely important. It is not advisable to go out and buy sheep, pigs, goats, chickens, geese, etc. in one go. Introduce one species at a time and gain knowledge, confidence and experience before embarking on the next. Most commercial farmers focus on just one species, with knowledge passed down through generations – and even then, they can come up against problems.

When keeping more than one species on a smallholding, your land management, husbandry and DIY skills will be tested regularly – all the more reason to set up slowly and methodically. Learning and observing each species individually will give you the chance to use and trust your common sense. For example, you will discover that cows and sheep work well together, as cows graze long grass and sheep prefer short grass, so they will happily share a grazing area. However, keeping chickens and pigs together is not a good idea at all: in fact, you can expect to have a few chicken casualties if you do this, as the pigs will eat the chickens. Housing and feeding requirements vary greatly from animal to animal – these are covered in the individual sections later in the book.

The best advice I can give you is to move slowly, learn as much as you can at every stage, and enjoy it. You will not always get things right, but you will progress and, as you do so, you will discover that there is often no such thing as a right or wrong way of doing things. The basic rules may be constant, but all animals behave differently and no two pieces of land are ever the same – so little details will always have to be tweaked along the way. As your knowledge and confidence grow, so too will your crops and livestock.

RIGHT: A couple of Highland Cows enjoying their meal.

the good life vs. real life

The 'good life' seems to be something a lot of people aspire to in today's hectic world, and smallholding and self-sufficiency are becoming extremely popular. Many people view this lifestyle as a dream – the idea of collecting freshly laid eggs on a sunny day and watching animals grazing happily inspires a sense of calm and contentment. However, let me shatter that illusion. If you do it right, there can be moments just like this, but 'the good life' doesn't mean 'the easy life' – far from it.

Do not be under any illusion: it is both physically and mentally demanding, and you will have a huge responsibility to your livestock. You need to have a passion for the land and its animals, and not be put off by bad weather and hard work.

Although you really cannot beat the sense of contentment that a smallholding can bring, you must remember: the weather isn't always sunny, the crops are often eaten by the wildlife and the livestock are not always well behaved. With smallholdings, you need to have a 'be prepared for anything' attitude. You can almost guarantee that, if you have planned a night out, a pig will escape or a goat will fall ill. Many times I have been dressed to impress and ready to head out only to find myself donning my wellie boots and headtorch to sort out a problem. Does

this put me off? No – and, in fact, it usually leads to a good story to tell when I do eventually make it to wherever I was planning to go!

Despite (or perhaps because of) the hard work, becoming a smallholder is one of the most rewarding things I have ever done. Getting back to basics is extremely satisfying – there is nothing quite like cooking a meal with eggs, meat or milk produced by the animals you have raised.

When I talk to my friends who farm, no one complains about their problems; we all accept the challenges of our chosen lifestyle, and we learn from them.

With passion (and bloody hard work), the rewards are extraordinary and you will be able to run a productive, happy smallholding. The land you purchase might not be the best when you buy it, but there are many things you can do to help it become productive (see Chapter 2, Cultivating your Land). Remember that there is a solution to every problem you will encounter – be calm, think it through and try to find a solution. That is, after all, the best way to learn. If you choose to cry and admit defeat you will not succeed.

In this book I will share my experience and try to give you a real insight into living the 'good life'.

1

BEFORE
YOU GET
STARTED

Turning your smallholding from a dream into a reality is not an easy process. There is a lot of hard work ahead and it can seem extremely daunting. However, if you work slowly and methodically and allow yourself plenty of time to learn the ropes, you can achieve your dream.

This chapter covers some of the practical matters that you will need to address before you even begin to consider bringing animals onto your land.

how much work is involved?

There is always something that needs doing on a smallholding. Animals need looking after and feeding every day, crops need tending, and fences, buildings and machinery need to be maintained. And these are just your everyday jobs! Add to that the additional work created by lambing time, routine vaccinations, worming, foot trimming, escaping animals, trips to the abattoir... I think it's safe to say there is a lot of work and it is on-going – every day, all year round. When you have animals, you can't just miss a day because you're tired. On some days there will be more jobs to do than time allows, and on other days you may find the time to enjoy a cup of tea with the sun shining, and admire your hard work. Precious moments like this are enough to recharge your batteries and enthuse you once more.

Winter is always hard – the shorter days and changeable weather present a whole host of new challenges. But I love the buzz when autumn starts settling in: chopping logs, stocking the barn with gorgeous-smelling hay, harvesting sloe berries from the hedgerows and bottling batches of sloe vodka (the perfect winter warmer!), the fire in the evenings as you shower and rest your aching body knowing all your animals are safe, well fed and watered. The feeling is hard to describe. Your cheeks glow, your feet are toasty and your mind is relaxed – total contentment. Just make sure you approach winter with the right attitude, remembering that you need to put in hard work in order to get the reward of blissful evenings – and never underestimate the need for warm, comfortable, waterproof clothing!

the size of your smallholding

A smallholding is usually thought of as a piece of land between 1 and 10 acres in size (4,000–40,000 sq m), but there is no legal description so the term is open to interpretation. In general terms, though, any piece of land that is 10 acres or above is classed as a farm, although the term 'farm' is usually used when the land is profitable. There are, however, pieces of land known as farms because they used to be working land, even though they are now just family homes.

The size of land that you'll need varies enormously depending on what you want to achieve. A large garden, if well utilised, can be surprisingly productive, with space to grow an abundance of vegetables and fruit, as well as accomodate chickens,

ducks, quails and rabbits. If conditions are right, there could also be space for a beehive for honey. The smaller your space, the more carefully you will need to plan to make sure it is well used. Sometimes, the less land you have, the more productive it can be.

A couple of acres (8,000 sq m) would be sufficient space for you to keep a few pigs, goats, sheep and chickens, with enough room for a decent vegetable patch – as long as the land is kept healthy through crop rotation (see pages 38–39).

Between 5 and 10 acres (20,000–40,000 sq m) will mean you have enough space to grow your own fodder crops (see page 38) and keep a few cows comfortably. It will also making resting and rotating the land much simpler.

LEFT: Keeping tools neatly in the right place saves time in the long run.

fencing

Fencing is an expensive operation, but it is one of the most important aspects of running your smallholding responsibly. When you have livestock, it is imperative that you construct suitable fences and maintain them correctly. It is your responsibility to keep your animals safe and under control – even people who love animals are going to be furious if they find your cows trampling their rose garden or your sheep holding up the traffic. You need to know what fencing is suitable for the animals you are going to keep.

All boundaries need to be properly secured and regularly maintained. There are a number of options open to you when it comes to fencing.

post and rail fencing

This is a very expensive but aesthetically pleasing option. It is made up of wooden posts with horizontal rails nailed onto them. The height and number of rails required will vary depending on the livestock. Common sense prevails here: a pig is not going to jump over a high fence, but could walk underneath if a large gap is left at the bottom; goats are agile and, depending on the breed, can easily push through a gap between rails; and chickens will just walk through, so will require post and netting/mesh fencing (see right). Electric fencing placed along the top will deter horses and cattle from rubbing themselves on the fencing, which can damage and sometimes snap the wood. Stock wire can be attached for extra security (see photo, top left).

post and wire fencing

This is a cheaper option, where posts are placed deeply and evenly into the ground and wire is stretched tightly between them. It is very important that the wire is stretched taut – particularly with goats – but all animals will stick their heads through the gaps between the wires! For some reason the grass is always greener on the other side. Again, you can use electric fencing to protect the posts, but I advise you to avoid barbed wire. It does work, but it can cause awful injuries to a determined or spooked animal – or a careless human.

post and netting/mesh fencing

There are different kinds of wire netting/mesh on the market suitable for containing different animals. All have different-sized holes and are different heights – obviously sheep netting is not going to contain chickens! Netting needs to be attached tightly to your posts and, if you wish, can be strengthened with rails. If you are keeping pigs this way, it really helps to put a single strand of electric fencing about 15cm off the ground to stop strong snouts pushing up on the wire and damaging the fencing. Animals will always be testing your boundaries – I don't know whether it is to keep us on our toes or to keep themselves amused, but it is a very good idea to do a quick check of your fencing every day.

CLOCKWISE FROM TOP LEFT: Post and rail fencing with stock wire attached; electric poultry fencing; a Faverolle hen perching on fencing; Large Black piglets peeking out of their stock-fenced pen; three strands of electric wire attached to poles using plastic spacers makes an ideal system for containing pigs.

electric fencing

Test Fence Regularly!

This is an extremely good way of containing your livestock and great for creating grazing areas in the short term as it is so easy to set up and move around. Moving your grazing areas allows you to avoid overgrazing your ground, enabling the land to rest and in turn keeping it healthy. However, I do think that the main boundaries of your property should be enclosed by a more permanent fence for peace of mind.

Electric fencing is very versatile and, once you have had it for a while, you'll find it extremely easy to use. When I first started using electric fencing, it really scared me – I'd been brought up in a house with particularly bad wiring and, as a child, was repeatedly told to never touch electrics! However, when used correctly, electric fencing is perfectly safe, and nothing beats it when it comes to keeping your animals safe. It provides an effective physical and psychological barrier that keeps livestock in and predators out.

Understanding how electric fencing works makes it less intimidating. A pulsed electric current travels along the wire from an energiser that is grounded. When the animal touches the wire, it completes the circuit and the animal receives a short, sharp shock. The shock is safe, but is enough to make sure the animal avoids touching the fence again.

You can buy kits that are suitable for chickens, rabbit, sheep and deer, as well as for horses and cattle. Lightweight electric netting is easy to use and move, but should not be used for horned animals as they can become entangled. Buy from a suitable specialist supplier; they will give you help and advice if needed. Electric fences are very easy to set up and will come with step-by-step instructions.

You can run your fencing off the mains power, but you will require a mains energiser unit, which needs to be installed inside a building by a qualified electrician. This does mean that you can use the fencing only near the power outlet, unless you have a very long extension cable. Battery-operated energisers, which use rechargeable batteries, are more commonly used, as they are completely portable. You can also buy solar panels that recharge the batteries, which are really effective.

Although all fencing needs regular maintenance, it's especially important to maintain electric fencing. Fallen leaves and branches or overgrown grass can ground the current, making it less effective. Test your fencing regularly; specially made electric fence testers are cheap to buy, extremely safe and easy to use.

A lot of people ask if electric fencing is safe for children. It is – like animals, they will touch it only once. Well, actually, that may not be strictly true for my children… when I first got the electric fence, they would dare each other to touch it, and push each other towards it – all kids do! But after teasing each other for an hour or so they became fully aware of the function of the fence and could empathise with the animal receiving their first shock. Despite this, I would, of course, strongly advise children not to play near or touch the electric fencing.

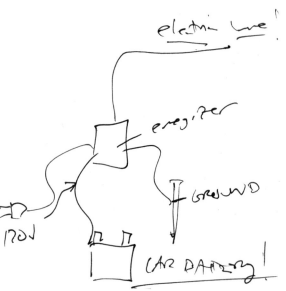

electric line
energiser
GROUND
120v
CAR BATTERY!

CLOCKWISE FROM BOTTOM LEFT: The battery; the energiser unit; electric fencing keeping poultry safe and contained.

hurdles

Hurdles are pieces of lightweight portable fencing. They are fantastic for making temporary pens for larger animals (poultry will not be contained by them). They can also be used to temporarily block gaps in hedges in an emergency. These days they are mostly made of metal and are easy to link together to make any shape or size pen. Some people use them as permanent pens, but this is an expensive option compared with normal fencing – they are designed to be mobile and this is the best way to use them. They are also useful for making corrals or tunnels, which animals can be driven through – ideal when it comes to shearing sheep, milking cows, or getting animals into trailers. If you have a good supply of hazel or willow on your smallholding, you might like to learn the traditional craft of weaving wattle hurdles.

RIGHT: Metal hurdles used in my barn to create a temporary pen for the sheep.

gates

Gates are a crucial factor to consider when you are fencing your property. Think about how you will be using the space and work out where the best places for gates will be. It's also important to consider which way you want them to open. Gates opening into your field are safer, especially if the field opens directly onto a road. Animals will often run towards you as you approach (they are just coming to say hello, and probably hoping you're going to feed them!), so having your gates opening inwards will help to stop them from rushing out of the field.

Metal gates tend to be lighter and don't require as much maintenance, although traditional wooden gates do look prettier. As with fences, you need to consider the different types of animals you are trying to contain, and ensure that the gates are appropriate for them.

TIP: The best advice I can give if you have never fenced before is to get a professional to do it – it's not as easy as it looks! You can watch and learn the skills for future projects; alternatively, you can go on a fencing course. Effective fencing will save you a huge amount of time and hassle and it really is worth investing in it properly.

RIGHT: A metal gate being guarded by my Embden geese.

buildings

Although the smallholding lifestyle is all about the great outdoors, buildings are essential. In each of the individual animal sections, I have explained what kind of building, if any, is needed for that animal. But you must also have enough secure indoor space to store your tools, machinery and feed. Do not underestimate the amount of space you will need.

Storage for feed and hay must be free from damp and, ideally, vermin–proof. Not only do vermin eat the food, they also carry diseases. So make sure the storage building is secure, sheltered from rain but well ventilated, and keep the feed and hay off the ground – most people use pallets for this purpose.

Storage for equipment needs to be secure and, especially when it comes to machinery, free from damp. Crime in the country is on the increase, so expensive tools should be kept safely under lock and key – a sad sign of the times.

LEFT: British Saanen Goats running to greet their owner, with a barn in the background. BOTTOM: Three Embden geese, 'Honker', my African goose, and a variety of Call Ducks standing in front of a stable.

outbuildings

If you are lucky enough to have some outbuildings on your smallholding, look after them. If they are wooden, treat the timber annually and repair them as soon as you see a problem – it is much easier and cheaper to repair a small fault than a large one.

If your smallholding has no existing outbuildings, try to find out why the previous owner didn't build any. It might be that buildings were just not needed for what the land was used for, but it could also be that there was a problem with planning permission, so it's important to consider this. It is possible to buy second–hand buildings, such as stables, field shelters and barns, which can often be dismantled and moved to a new location – just make sure you have permission to erect them.

field shelters

As the name suggests, this is a structure to provide shelter in a field. It would generally be a covered structure, open on one side, and with no floor. You can get both permanently fixed field shelters and mobile ones. These shelters are really useful for grazing animals and provide protection from the elements. They can also double up as lambing sheds with the use of hurdles.

pole barns

A pole barn is a simple shed that can be erected easily; essentially poles are set into the ground, secured together and then the top and sides are covered. Depending on the size, pole barns can be used for storage of machinery or feed, or overwintering animals. Think carefully about where you position your pole barn – you don't want it to be vulnerable to flooding or strong winds.

polytunnels

Polytunnels are growing in popularity and are used not only for growing vegetables but also for livestock. They are ideal for use during lambing time, and I've used one to rear turkeys for Christmas. You can also use them for chickens and ducks, although these birds will also need housing so that they are secure at night. Polytunnels are much cheaper than permanent structures and can be taken down or have the covering taken off when not needed. Depending on their size, they are quite easy to put up yourself.

There are also plenty of options for creating makeshift buildings as and when they are needed. In an emergency I have used straw bales to build walls for a shelter and popped a corrugated sheet on top;

it worked perfectly while I was rearing some turkeys. My sister built a lean-to along the back of her stables and managed to store 200 bales of hay perfectly; tarpaulins were tacked to the sides to keep the rain out but still allow air through, while pallets were laid down to keep the hay off the ground. Use your imagination – as long as a shelter does the job that it's intended for and it is safe for both you and your livestock, then I am all for improvising.

ABOVE: Badger Face Welsh Mountain ewes that are due to lamb being housed in a polytunnel – note the lower part is meshed for ventilation. **RIGHT:** A water container collecting water from the field shelter roof.

water

One of the most important commodities needed for livestock and crops is water, so it's among the first things you should consider when you are getting ready to set up your smallholding.

Do you have a mains supply of water in the fields? It is no fun carting buckets of water to and fro every day. If you do not have a mains supply (in fact, even if you do), you should collect rainwater. Water prices are increasing, so why pay out when you can collect your own? Place water butts or large water tanks near a stable or barn. Avoid clear containers, as sunlight will soon cause algae to build up. The best option is to have your collection tanks underground. You can do this yourself, but if you haven't got a digger it will take a long time to dig an adequate hole, so you might want to consider getting someone in to install the collection tanks for you. Putting guttering on your buildings to collect water for the butts is simple – if I can do it, anyone can! Just remember that gravity will come into play, so ensure your gradient is correct. I once spent a couple of days setting up guttering along a field shelter only to discover that the shelter was on a slight slope, and I had placed the water butt on the higher side! Experience is everything.

Another option is to drill a borehole. This is a very deep but narrow hole, which is dug until it reaches an underground spring. You will need to have a survey to see if your site is suitable. In the UK, the British Geological Survey (BGS) can carry out a water borehole prognosis report for you for a fee. This information is then passed on to the Environment Agency (in England and Wales), who will tell you whether you need to apply for a licence. It really depends on how much water you will be using as to whether this is a viable option – if you're operating on a smaller scale, a few water butts should be sufficient.

machinery and tools

The machinery that you'll need on your smallholding is, of course, entirely dependent on what you are planning to do there. You don't need a tractor if you only have 1 acre, but if you have 10, it would be useful. A ride–on lawn mower is good for up to 2 acres (8,000 sq m) of land, although when we first moved to our smallholding my husband managed to cope with a petrol lawn mower, much to the amusement of the locals! (We have since upgraded to a ride–on mower.) That said, we were planning to graze our land the following year with sheep and had worked out a rotation system to eliminate the need for grass cutting. Strimmers are useful to keep hedges under control, as well as rotavators for preparing the ground for growing vegetables.

All-terrain or rough-terrain vehicles are a must if you have bumpy or rough land – a quad bike with a trailer is great for ferrying feed to your livestock in

the furthest fields, and some have attachments that can allow you to harrow, for example.

All machinery is dangerous if not used correctly, so training, particularly with tractors, is a must. Chainsaws should be used with extreme care and protective clothing is needed with these. The list of machinery goes on, but remember you can hire machinery and sometimes it can be cheaper or more efficient to pay someone with the correct equipment to come in and do the job for you.

My advice is to buy good–quality agricultural tools. Attend farm sales, as your equipment really needs to be up to the job and cheap domestic items just won't last.

THE SMALLHOLDER'S HANDBOOK

the smallholder's essential toolkit

Many people (including me) overlook the basics, so here is my list of must-haves:

- sharp penknife (you will need it regularly, so keep it with you)
- torches (at least two, preferably waterproof), plus a couple of head torches so you can keep your hands free
- rechargeable batteries and a battery charger
- hammer
- drill
- wire cutters and wire
- spare fuses
- mobile phone

The list goes on! Just when you think you have all the tools you need, a job comes up that requires a tool that you do not have.

> **TIP:** If possible, buy brightly coloured equipment so when you drop it you can find it easily in the mud and grass.

security and insurance

With a smallholding, you never know what tomorrow will bring, so you must be as prepared as possible. Security and insurance are often overlooked until something happens and then it's a lesson learnt the very hard way. Rural crime is unfortunately on the increase, so security measures are essential. Machinery, tools and livestock all need protecting.

- Keep machinery out of view and preferably locked up when not in use, and don't leave keys in the vehicle. This may sound like common sense but when you are out and about in the fields, you can easily be distracted as another job beckons.

- Never leave tools lying about.

- Perimeter fencing should be secure – a padlock is an inconvenience to thieves.

- Growing prickly hedges can be a deterrent, as can keeping noisy guinea fowl and geese. Make sure all buildings are secure.

- Dogs on smallholdings not only work as burglar alarms but some also keep vermin at bay and help round up animals.

Making sure you have the correct insurance for your smallholding is imperative. Not only do you have to insure your machinery, tools, outbuildings and livestock against theft and damage, you also need to get public liability insurance – what happens if one of your animals escapes and causes an accident or injures someone? You must also be covered if you hope to visit agricultural shows with livestock or take your produce to farmers' markets. In addition, if you have any workers on your land, or a public footpath crossing your fields, you need to make sure you have the appropriate insurance.

Make sure your policies cover all your needs and shop around for a good deal. Your chosen insurance company should advise you on what is needed – just make sure you inform them of everything you have on your land, and what you plan to do with it.

2
CULTIVATING
YOUR LAND

Before your land can become productive, you need to put work into it. Most smallholders use their land for growing crops as well as keeping animals – in fact, when planned and managed correctly, much of your animals' feed can come from the land you already own.

It's easy for the quality of your land to slip if you don't look after it well. Mistakes like over-grazing can be damaging to your land as well as your livestock. So take some time to familiarise yourself with your natural resources; learn about the kind of soil you have, and think about how your smallholding is laid out. This will help you to get the very best from what you have.

types of soil

Soil changes from area to area and each type is suited to different crops and uses. If you are planning to grow crops, your first step should be to find out what soil type you have, as it will determine what you can grow successfully. There are five main soil types: sandy, clay, silt, loam and chalky (see right). To get an idea of your soil type, observe what your neighbours or local farmers are growing on their land.

Plants also need mineral elements to thrive; the most important ones are: nitrogen (N), phosphorus (P) and potassium (K). You can tell which of these elements are present or lacking in your soil by looking at the plants growing in it. Nitrogen supports leaf growth and if the plants don't have enough it can cause a yellowing of the leaves. Phosphorus helps healthy root growth; not enough is indicated by poor growth and dark or dull yellow leaves. Potassium is needed for strong roots, flowers and fruit as well as providing good disease resistance. Check your soil's pH levels and nutrient levels regularly – you can buy kits at your local garden centre for this.

Sandy soil is gritty in texture and low in nutrients, so needs plenty of organic matter added.

Clay soil is sticky and heavy; break it up by adding organic matter and digging over regularly.

Silt soil can easily become compacted – it contains more nutrients than sandy soil and it holds water better.

Loam is the ideal soil type and provides a strong start to most plants – add organic matter if you are cultivating every year.

Chalky soil will need organic matter added, and you should select plants that grow well in it.

the lay of the land

There are some important questions you need to ask when considering how to use your land.

• Is your land rocky and full of stones? If so, you can rule out growing crops. It also makes finding a spot to put in fencing posts difficult.

• Does your land flood? This could mean that some areas are unusable during certain times of the year.

• Is your land sheltered or exposed to the wind? How sunny is it? Which direction does it face? If you keep animals on land that is exposed to wind, shelter will need to be provided and care taken when choosing your livestock. Crops also need shelter – planting hedges to protect them from prevailing winds will help. Similarly, if the field where you would like to keep your animals is very sunny without any natural shade, you will need to put up shelters to create shade for them.

• Do any public footpaths run past, or even through your fields? This could make keeping livestock troublesome as there may be walkers passing through, so you will have to make sure that your animals will not disturb them – and vice versa.

• Do you have water on your land? If not, you will need to work out how to sort out a water supply if you want to keep livestock and grow crops (see page 29).

• Are access and security good?

These factors will have an impact on what you can do with your land. Observe your surrounding area and get to know the locals – by drinking in the local pub! Picking people's brains will help you come up with solutions. As I said before, every piece of land is different. When I first moved to my smallholding in the summer, all was great – then came the rain, and my lovely field began to flood. By talking to my neighbours, I discovered that there was a water gulley running down the side of my field. It was on the other side of my boundary and had not been cleared for a rather long time. We cleared the brambles and re-dug the gulley and our field drained beautifully.

ploughing

Ploughing is an essential part of growing crops. It will loosen and aerate the soil. It also controls weeds. If you have compacted soil, it is difficult for water to get through and seedlings will struggle to establish their roots and grow. Compaction can be caused by heavy rainfall, animals' hooves and heavy machinery. Ploughing loosens the ground so it can 'breathe' and let water in.

However, ploughing or digging to the same depth year after year can cause hardpan to form. Hardpan is a dense layer under the soil that makes it difficult for roots and water to penetrate; the result is waterlogging, which will kill your crops. Treating the problem involves first ploughing to loosen the soil and then breaking up the hardpan with a spade, which is back–breaking work.

Dig over your land in the winter – the freezing and thawing process helps break up soil, making it easier for you. It is also essential to pick out any weeds as you go; a freshly dug area is a magnet for weeds. Another trick is to enlist the help of your livestock. Pigs do a very good job of turning over land and they fertilise as they go. Chickens can also help on the veg patch – they will clear pests, scratch soil and fertilise remarkably quickly.

BELOW: Pigs can make very quick work of clearing land of weeds, and also do a great job of turning over and fertilising the soil.

crop rotation

Crop rotation is the practice of growing specific groups of vegetables on different parts of the vegetable plot each year. As well as growing crops that you like to eat, make sure that you select ones that are suitable for your soil and climate. I tend to grow produce that cannot be bought cheaply locally and always opt for varieties that are reasonably disease-resistant – this makes life a little easier.

A herb garden is a must-have – not only are herbs wonderful to cook with, many are fantastic for livestock as well. Rosemary is a great anti-inflammatory/antiseptic; and thyme can be an excellent remedy for excess mucus when added to bedding and feed.

There are other vegetables you may choose to grow for your animals as well as yourself. Garlic helps boost the immune system, so is great to feed to animals at times of stress, such as shearing time or if you are moving them. I love rosehip: not only does it look gorgeous, it is also a great source of vitamin C. Nettles are good for humans in soup and tea, and, when dried, they are rich in protein, which makes them a

great addition to animal feed in the winter months (see page 40). You can also grow what are known as 'fodder crops', which can be used to help keep your animal feed bills down in winter when pasture is poor and the animals can't graze as much. Kale, beetroot, turnips, swede and rape are all great for this. If you have only a couple of acres and want to use them for animals, growing fodder crops isn't really an option, but you might have a neighbour who would be willing to let you grow some on their land in return for some produce. It is always worth asking, or you will never know!

Whatever you choose, growing the same crop year after year in the same location can deplete the soil of important nutrients, making the ground less fertile and healthy. Humans need a balanced diet to keep us fit and well, and rest to give us energy, and the ground's needs are not dissimilar. Different crops have different nutrient requirements, so changing the ground that the crops are grown on every year reduces the chances of particular soil deficiencies occurring, as the balance of nutrients removed will balance out over time. Rotating the crops that you grow from year to year also helps to stop the build-up of crop-specific pests and diseases.

In order to rotate crops effectively, they should be grouped according to their needs. The four main groups are brassicas, legumes, onions and roots, and potatoes.

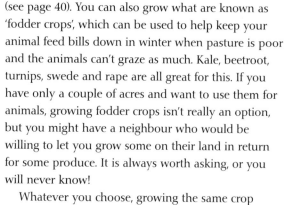

- Brassicas: Brussels sprouts, cauliflowers, cabbages, kale, radishes, broccoli
- Legumes: peas, broad beans, French and runner beans
- Onions and roots: onions, garlic, shallots, leeks
- Potato family: potatoes, tomatoes, peppers and aubergines

Crops such as courgettes, pumpkins, squashes, marrows, cucumbers, runner beans, salads and sweetcorn can be grown wherever is convenient – just avoid growing them in the same place each year. Although members of the potato family, peppers and aubergines can be grown anywhere in rotation. Perennial vegetables, such as rhubarb and asparagus, do not fit into crop rotation as they just keep growing and can stay in the same spot for many years.

The most common plan is to do a four-year rotation based on four sections; every year, the crops are moved round to the next section, so that brassicas follow legumes, potatoes follow brassicas, onions and roots follow potatoes, and legumes follow onions and roots.

YEAR 1
Section one: Legumes
Section two: Brassicas
Section three: Potato family
Section four: Onions and roots

YEAR 2
Section one: Brassicas
Section two: Potato family
Section three: Onions and roots
Section four: Legumes

YEAR 3
Section one: Potato family
Section two: Onions and roots
Section three: Legumes
Section four: Brassicas

YEAR 4
Section one: Onions and roots
Section two: Legumes
Section three: Brassicas
Section four: Potato family

The main focus of this book is on keeping animals, and so I have not gone into great detail about growing crops. However, I would advise you to approach this in the same way as you approach caring for your animals – start small, learn as you go, and be ready for surprises!

Land rotation does not only apply to crops – it's important practice for the land used by your animals, too. Put very simply, rotating your land keeps the land clean and enables it to rest and regrow so that there is always grazing for your animals. If you keep animals on the same land for a long time, it will end up overgrazed, filled with animal waste and ultimately unproductive. Land will always benefit from having no animals on it for a few months of the year – this is easy to achieve if you do not have too many animals for the size of your smallholding, so always factor in land rotation when you are working out how many animals you have space for. That's the golden rule for land management – rotate regularly.

LEFT: Maize, a favourite with poultry. **ABOVE:** Pumpkins are easy to grow, taste great, and the seeds make a natural wormer for poultry.

weed control

Weeds are a constant problem and need to be dealt with regularly to prevent them becoming unmanageable. Weeds will compete with your crops for nutrients and water and can quickly choke small plants and seedlings. They also encourage pests and diseases. Some plants cope with weeds better than others: for example, potatoes and squashes have dense foliage that helps suppress weeds, which cuts down on weeding – that said, there are only so many potatoes and squashes one can eat!

Weeding regularly not only gets rid of the weeds that are already growing, but can also prevent new weed seeds getting into your soil. If you choose to weed by pulling the weeds up by their roots, be careful not to pull your crops up too! Once you've pulled up a weed, drop it into a bucket or container and dispose of it – if you leave it lying on the ground, it may re-root or spread seeds. Ragwort is a particularly horrible weed that is found in fields. This needs to be removed using gloves as some people can suffer from an allergic reaction. Using a special ragwort fork to remove its roots is really the only way to get rid of this horrid weed – and it then needs to be burnt.

If you know your weeds, you may be able to use them to feed your animals – for example, hang bundles of stinging nettles for a couple of months to dry out, then add them to your chicken feed. Their nutrients provide a welcome boost during the hard winter months. Collecting nettles is easy – just cut about 30cm from the top, tie at the base into bunches and hang to dry in a barn or other indoor space. Remember to wear gloves and long sleeves to avoid being stung. Dock leaves are also great for chickens – I hang them up fresh in my chickens' runs to provide interest and vitamins.

I do not like using chemicals to tackle weeds. There are alternatives you can try, such as boiling water, vinegar sprayed neat onto the weed (although you do need to do this several times and in dry weather), salt, or sugar (mix this with hot chilli powder to stop other possible pests being tempted). Try mixing salt or sugar with water in a spray bottle to spray straight onto the weeds. Adding a little liquid soap will help the concoction stick to the weed.

pests and diseases

Pests and diseases that live in the soil tend to attack certain plant families over and over again. Rotating the crops causes the pests and diseases to decline while the host plants are elsewhere, which really helps to reduce the build-up of spores, eggs and pests, leading to healthy soil which means healthier vegetables.

Checking your plants and soil regularly for signs of pests and diseases is imperative. You can then remove and destroy adult pests and any eggs found by hand. Adding compost (see page 42) to your soil acts as a source of shelter and food for good microbes and helps them fight off fungal spores. Compost also helps prevent the ground becoming overly wet – moist conditions often help pests to breed.

Slugs and snails

Slugs can be disposed of with a jar full of beer. Bury it in the ground up to the rim. Slugs will go in for a drink and then drown. Placing board along the side of your vegetable patch will encourage snails to shelter there – all you have to do then is collect the snails at night and dispose of them.

Aphids

Aphids can be tackled with a homemade citrus spray. Place the rind of one lemon in a pint of hot water overnight, then transfer the water to a spray bottle and spray any aphids, paying particular attention to the underside of the plants leaves where they hide.

Remember, not all bugs are bad for crops, so do your research before heading out to kill them all.

TOP LEFT: Nettles drying in a barn. BOTTOM LEFT: Dried nettles mixed in with corn for an afternoon scratch feed for my hens. ABOVE: Runner beans.

compost

Composting speeds up the process of rot and decay so that waste is turned into a nutrient-rich food for your plants. It improves the soil structure, making drier soils retain more moisture and improving the structure of very wet soils, rather like adding cornflour to your sauces to obtain the perfect consistency. It keeps your soil's PH balance in check and helps to suppress plant disease. It is indeed the equivalent of our 'five-a-day' – without a proper diet, we would become sickly. Plants are no different, and soil is their food.

In addition, composting discourages many pests and can protect your plants from diseases. Composting also helps to keep a considerable amount of waste out of our landfill sites, where it produces harmful greenhouse gases such as methane, which damages the earth's atmosphere.

Food waste, such as fruit and vegetable peelings, tea bags and crushed eggshells, as well as grass cuttings, garden prunings cut into small pieces, newspaper and hay or straw manure (see opposite) will, in time, make a wonderful feed for your garden. Do not put cooked meat, fish bones or fat into your compost heap, as these will attract rats. Fallen leaves make fantastic compost but take much longer to rot down, so it's a good idea to keep a separate bin for leaf compost. An added benefit is that this will attract hedgehogs, which will keep slugs at bay.

Composting is very easy. You can buy plastic bins for composting from garden centres, but it is cheap and simple to build your own. My compost bins are made out of old wooden pallets with large-gauge chicken wire to keep out rats, and a clear plastic sheet on top to protect from rain. Whatever container you choose, it needs to be one that allows the waste to rot down. You should position your compost bin in a sunny spot, as warmth is an important part of the process. Place it on bare soil so that insects can gain access. This also helps with aeration and drainage, which are important for successful composting.

As you add your waste materials to the compost bin, they will begin to break down. This part of the process can generate a surprising amount of warmth – the middle of a compost heap can get quite hot, and people often refer to the process as 'cooking'.

If you are gathering material for your compost gradually, cover each addition with a sprinkling of soil. This helps to stop the compost bin getting too smelly, and also discourages vermin.

Every month or so, mix your compost with a spade or garden fork. This will help it to break down and moves it around, bringing the parts of the compost that have been sitting on the edges of the bin into the middle, so you get a more even compost. You can get rotary composters that you turn to make mixing easier, but this isn't necessary.

Compost is ready to use when it is a very dark brown colour, is crumbly in texture and has a lovely, earthy smell. Using compost is easy – for seedlings, mix 1 part compost with 3 parts soil. To help established plants, place a layer of compost on top of the soil – it is also great sprinkled on top of your lawn. When it comes to your vegetable plot, dig as much compost as you like into the soil.

Build Compost Bin with Pallets! ⊕
Build cover for the Bin!

GOAL: CREATE GOOD ORGANIC COMPOST! ⊕

manure

Adding manure to your compost increases the nitrogen levels, adds
microorganisms and increases the speed at which your compost
breaks down. I use manure from my chicken houses, taking both
the straw bedding and the droppings to compost. You need to mix
manure with leaves or bedding to get a balanced compost. All
livestock manure can be used (I find chicken manure gives the best
results) but, as mentioned, it is best mixed with leaves or straw.
Collecting manure is easy: either use a spade or put on some gloves
and just pick it up. If you have empty vegetable beds over the
winter, you can place manure directly on top, cover with a tarpaulin
and leave until the spring when you can dig it in.

pasture

The type and quality of your pasture is really important. Pasture is any material being grazed by livestock and it is the cheapest way to feed them. Good pasture is essential for healthy animals; if your pasture is poor, your animals' feed will be poor.

Pasture consists of grass–legumes (such as clover or alfalfa), grass and forbs (miscellaneous flowering plants, including dandelions). All contain nutrients that come from the soil and in turn nourish your animal. With good management and rotation, your pastures should thrive.

The animals work the pasture for you: their hooves aerate the soil and their urine and faeces act as fertiliser. If you take animals out of a pasture it will change – weeds take over and trees begin to grow.

Looking at the land in your area will determine what is best to grow. If there is no grass, just weeds, you will need to re-seed the land with grass seeds. Do not allow livestock to graze the land until grass seedlings are well established – the rule of thumb is to wait until they are about 15cm tall.

Pasture can also be used to grow hay, which can

then be stored as feed over the winter. There are several hay types: alfalfa is best mown when in bud, while clover is lovely but not ideal for the novice as it is harder to dry in the field. Straight grass hay dries more easily, so is a better option if you are new to haymaking. Weather plays a huge part in haymaking, as you need several dry days to cut, dry and bale. I love haymaking time, as there is a real buzz among the farmers to get everything done, with everyone helping out – and when it is finally all over, the drinks flow freely!

Cutting your hay can be as simple as mowing with a ride–on mower with the cutter set on high or using a tractor and cutter, then forking and raking the cuttings over in the field in rows in order to dry out. When the hay is fully dry you can tie it into bundles. If you have a tractor and a baler and turner, you can do it yourself but it's perfectly feasible to just ask a local farmer to come and cut, turn and bale it for you. You then need to use a trailer to move your hay bales to an aerated barn for storage. Hay will keep for about 12 months. You can still use it after this time, but it can become dusty, so soaking it in water before giving it to livestock will be advantageous. You do need to be fit as it really is hard work – but fun nonetheless!

LEFT: Luke's beautiful Irish Moiled Cows grazing. RIGHT: Fresh hay is enjoyed when grass is in short supply.

3
KEEPING ANIMALS
THE ESSENTIALS

Every day, I feel very privileged to be able to experience the benefits of raising animals on a smallholding. Every day, my livestock make me smile, and create a very positive and calming effect on my well-being. That said, every day, I usually find several new bruises and aches from all the manual labour involved in animal care!

The joy of keeping livestock will have a positive effect on your own mental well-being, but you need to make sure that you focus on their mental well-being, too. You need to have empathy with your charges. It is not enough to provide them with feed and water – they need to have a happy and safe living environment, and be treated with care and respect. In fact, I always say you should simply treat your animals as you would like to be treated. Not only is it the right thing to do from a moral point of view, it will also lead to a more successful smallholding, as a happy, contented animal is usually a healthy, productive one.

the five freedoms

As a livestock farmer you must ensure that you meet all the relevant animal welfare requirements. In the UK, the Farm Animal Welfare Committee recommends you follow the Five Freedoms for farm livestock. These were first developed following a UK government report, but have since been adopted by animal welfare organisations across Europe and the rest of the world, including the World Organisation for Animal Health. The Five Freedoms state that animals should be given:

Freedom from hunger and thirst

Clean water should be available at all times and food should be adequate to maintain full health and vigour.

Freedom from discomfort

Provide an appropriate environment with shelter and a comfortable, clean bed.

Freedom from pain and injury or disease

Make sure you have adequate knowledge to prevent disease or provide rapid diagnosis and treatment.

Freedom to express normal behaviour

Give them enough space to jump, run and scratch. Ensure your animals have access to everything they need and the company of their own kind.

Freedom from fear and distress

Provide them with conditions and treatment that don't cause them mental suffering. In other words, as I said previously, treat them as you would like to be treated.

ABOVE: Access to clean, fresh water is one of the Five Freedoms.

When I consider the trust that animals place in us, and the food and joy they provide us with, it seems clear that nobody should keep animals if they cannot give them what they need and deserve.

LEFT: Goats are very affectionate and enjoy our company. ABOVE: A stunning Rhode Island Red Cockerel enjoying the space he needs to scratch around.

legal guidelines

What you intend to use your land for will determine whether you need to be registered as an agricultural holding. As a general rule, if you want to keep legged animals, such as goats, pigs, sheep or cows, or a large number of birds, you will need to register (see below). If, on the other hand, you want to keep only a few chickens, grow vegetables and maybe have a couple of beehives, you do not.

The legal guidelines below apply in the UK – in other countries, you should check your own government guidelines.

CPH number

If you wish to keep legged animals (pigs, cows, sheep, etc.) or a substantial number of poultry (over 50 birds), the first thing you need to do is obtain a County Parish Holding number, or CPH number for short.

When I first embarked on this myself, I was extremely daunted, as paperwork is really not my forte. However, it is very simple, so do not despair! In the UK, you just need to contact the Rural Payments Agency (RPA – see Resources pages 218–219); all it takes is a simple phone call and you will be sent the relevant paperwork.

A CPH number is used for administrative purposes. It makes tracing owners easier in the event of disease outbreak, and you also need it to buy or sell livestock, to move them on and off your holding, when ordering identification tags, and for several official documents – so your adventure really cannot begin until you have this. A CPH number is made up of 9 digits: the first 2 indicate the county you live in, the next 3 indicate the parish and the last 4 are your actual holding number for your smallholding.

unique herd/flock number

Once you have your CPH number, you need to obtain your unique herd/flock number. To get this, you need to contact your local Animal & Plant Health Agency (APHA) office, who you can find through the Department for Environmental, Food and Rural Affairs (Defra) website (see Resources pages 218–219). You will need to inform them of the animals you wish to keep, and they will then issue you with your herd/flock number, which you need for movement and slaughter purposes.

The number will need to be on all ear tags (or slap marks for pigs), which are then worn by the animals leaving the holding, whether for slaughter, going to a new home or travelling to market or a show. You can order your identification tags for your animals from several different companies, but they will all ask for your CPH number and your herd/flock number. Details of identification and movement regulations for specific animals will be covered in their relevant chapters.

CLOCKWISE FROM BOTTOM LEFT: A goat with a metal ear tag; lambs with their mums; a cow with a plastic ear tag.

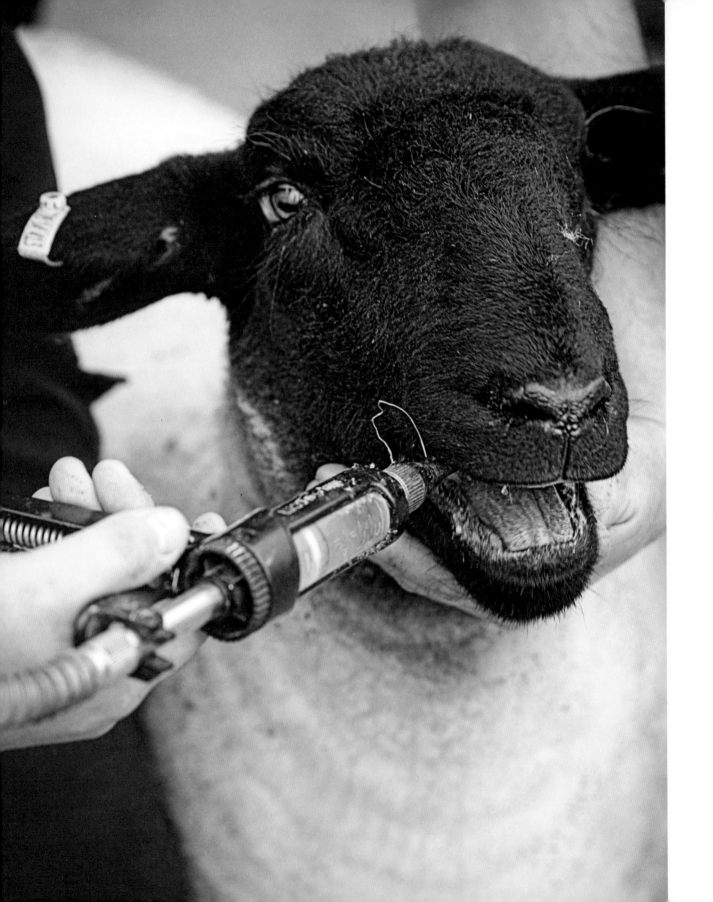

medicine and record-keeping

I'll cover medicines and health issues in more detail in the specific animal's chapters, but it's crucial to remember that any medicines used on your smallholding need to be recorded.

It is a legal requirement to keep records for three years and they should be available for inspection if required. Your local Trading Standards office (see Resources pages 218–219) can advise you on this and provide the relevant forms, which can either be completed online or as hard copies.

You need to record the following details:

- which animals you treated
- what type of medicine was used
- the date it was purchased
- the batch number
- the quantity used
- the dates of treatment
- any withdrawal periods
- who administered the medicine

When you record which animals have been treated, be sure to use their identification numbers, not their names, like Doris or Wilbur, which is what I did when I first started – luckily, my local Trading Standards man was patient and helpful!

When I speak to other smallholders, record keeping is always greeted with raised eyebrows and a sigh! However, we all know that record keeping is much more than just paperwork and red tape for the benefit of Defra and Trading Standards. Yes, it takes a little time to do and get used to, but it is an invaluable resource. Your records are there to help you provide the best care for your animals. It's a very good practice to get used to and will soon become second nature. I keep a lot of poultry and so I also keep records for worming and dealing with red mite, even though the products I use are organic – for example, I use Verm-X wormer, which is a totally natural, organic product. Organic products like this are not classed as medications, so I am not legally required to record them in this formal way, but I find it very useful to have the records as a reminder of when and how I have treated my animals. When you have lots of animals it is impossible to remember all dates, so use your records as reminders of when things are due.

If you ever notice several of your charges being ill with the same symptoms, you should always call a vet. Likewise, if a bird or animal is unwell for more than a few days, it should receive veterinary care.

Now that we have covered the basics, it's time to start exploring the different kinds of birds and livestock you can raise on your smallholding, and how best to care for them.

LEFT: A sheep being treated with a drench gun, which is an easy-to-use tool for administering worming mediation.

4

POULTRY
AND BIRDS

Keeping birds is a particular passion of mine. As well as being a source of gorgeous eggs and meat, I love the truly calming, therapeutic effect that observing them has on me. There's nothing better than watching their antics and listening to their contented clucks at the end of a hard day. If you are completely new to keeping animals, they are a great way to grow your confidence – it's much easier to handle a chicken than a cow!

You can keep different breeds of chickens together but, unless you are giving them a lot of space, I would advise keeping the size of chicken similar, as larger breeds can bully smaller ones.

Ducks and geese are also lovely to keep, and produce yummy eggs and meat. If you want to keep them in addition to poultry, they should have separate houses for sleeping in as they produce wet droppings, which quickly make the house damp – this is not good for chickens. Their feeding and watering areas should also be separate, as they are messy eaters and will soon turn any water source dirty, which is fine for them but not for poultry.

When it comes to choosing your birds, my advice is always the same: purchase good stock that have been well-reared on good-quality feed with sufficient space, and go to a reputable breeder who is happy to show you around and share their knowledge and experience with you.

bird flu

The very mention of bird flu makes every poultry keeper freeze with fear. Just remember, although we hear a lot about it, outbreaks are usually confined to very large commercial rearers or poorer parts of Asia, where people are living in confined areas with chickens. It's extremely unlikely that you would be hit by an outbreak on a smallholding, but the signs to look out for are:
• combs and wattles turning blue
• hens looking hunched and ill
• discharge from the beak and eyes

Death comes very quickly, and the disease has very high mortality rates. It is a notifiable disease, which means you are legally required to report any incident of it. If you ever have large numbers of birds dying, always contact your vet immediately.

chickens

Chickens are fantastic for beginners. They are usually the first port of call for a new smallholder and, in my opinion, chickens are also responsible for many of us yearning for the 'Good Life'; the early dreams of many wannabe smallholders often involve gathering eggs from their own hens.

There are so many backyard poultry keepers these days. Chickens do not require huge amounts of space and compared with other livestock are relatively cheap. People are also discovering just how much chickens give back – eggs, meat and lots of laughs! Once you have kept hens, they really do change your views of animals and the food you eat.

You do not need a CPH number to keep chickens, nor are you required to fill in moving licences. However, as I explained in Chapter 3, if you have more than 50 birds of any kind, you will need to register with Defra. It is also advisable, even if you have only a few birds, to keep a medicine/welfare book, just so you can keep track of worming, miting, etc (see page 53).

Before you begin, you need to decide what you want chickens for – meat, eggs, or both? Or maybe you want to keep some fancy birds to breed and sell on? Do your research and set up their housing properly before rushing out to buy your birds – you don't want to be feeding the fox through your poor planning.

RIGHT: A Salmon Faverolle cock overlooking his girls.

choosing a breed

Layers

If you want chickens solely for eggs, you really can't beat hybrids. These are chickens that have been bred by mixing different breeds together to produce one that excels at egg laying. Most are derived from well-known pure breeds like the Rhode Island Red, Leghorn, Maran or Sussex. You can purchase hybrids that lay white, blue, dark chocolate-brown and speckled eggs. They are very reliable layers, predictable by nature, and very easy to look after, making them great for first timers. They also rarely go broody (see box), although some do! They are very easy to source and available all year round. Some of the hybrid layers I would recommend are Black Rocks, Skylines, Maran Cuivres, Sussexes, Blacktails, Gold Lines, and Blue and White Leghorns.

If space is an issue, smaller chickens, known as bantams, still lay eggs while requiring less space and food than larger birds.

Purebred chickens do not lay as much as hybrids, but they do tend to live longer.

You can keep different breeds of chicken together but, unless you are giving them a lot of space, I would advise keeping the size of chicken similar, as larger breeds can bully smaller ones.

Meat birds

If you are raising chickens specifically for meat, go for broilers. If you can obtain them in your area, they are ideal meat birds. They are fast-growing (ready for slaughter in approximately 8 weeks) and produce big, tasty carcasses. They need very little, if any, hanging time (see page 130) and you can slaughter them at different times, as the males and females mature at varying rates. Don't be tempted to keep any to breed from, though; broilers are not future breeding stock, but the end product!

broody hens

When a hen is broody, it means she is at the stage of her reproductive cycle during which she incubates eggs – put very simply, a broody is a chicken that wants to be a mum! Some breeds are more given to broodiness than others (for example, Pekins and Silkies). You can tell a hen is broody because she will stay sitting in her nest box and not want to move. Her breast will be hot and she might have plucked out some of her feathers to make her nest. She will be wary if you approach her, and might fluff up her feathers to make herself look bigger, or even make a sort of growling noise. She might also give you a peck to warn you off.

If a broody hen is sitting on fertilised eggs, it's fine to leave her to it and let nature take its course (see page 71). If, however, you don't have a cockerel or you know she is sitting on unfertilised eggs, you need to remove them and try and break her broody habit. You can do this by moving her from her nest twice daily and putting her over by the food and water. She will probably return to the nest quite quickly, so remove the eggs before she returns.

If her habit proves hard to break, you might need to move her to a 'broody box' – a cage with a wire floor, which allows the air to circulate. This will cool her down, which should help to break her broodiness.

CLOCKWISE, FROM BOTTOM LEFT: An assortment of purebreed pullets including Gold Laced Brahmas, Silver Laced Brahmas, a Salmon Faverolle, a Japanese Booted Bantam cross, and the comically fluffy Frizzled Poland; an Orpington cock beginning his moult; and a Frizzle Pekin with her chicks.

A young male chicken is called a cockerel.
When he is fully grown (at about 1 year)
he is known as a cock.

If you breed purebred chickens and want to rear spare cockerels for the pot, you need to separate them from the girls. This gives the girls some peace and allows you to keep the meat birds in a restricted area. Don't be tempted to give them a vast space to run around in – they will end up with the legs and chest muscles of Mike Tyson. They may be good-looking boys, but their meat will be like leather! However, the area does need to be large enough for them to exhibit their natural behaviour, as laid out in the Five Freedoms (page 48). Purebred cockerels are usually ready to eat at around 6–10 months. In my opinion, they are much tastier than broilers. It's hard to describe the taste, exactly – let's just say they taste more chickeny!

If you choose to slaughter hens that have reached 'end of lay' (are now too old to lay eggs), they will require slow-cooking in casseroles rather than roasting, as their meat does tend to be dry and tough. Allowing suitable hanging time to tenderise the meat is a must (see page 130).

Once you have reared and tasted your own chicken there's no going back – it tastes absolutely delicious, nothing like the bland, flavourless meat in the supermarket. In addition, you're giving a bird the chance of a lovely, productive life that it might not have otherwise had.

For more information about slaughtering chickens, see pages 77–78.

Purebred dual-purpose birds

If you'd like to keep birds for meat and eggs, there are a number of breeds I can recommend.

Ixworth – These are bred to produce a white-skinned, broad-breasted carcass. An Ixworth will produce a good number of eggs – 160–200 per year. It is a very popular breed with smallholders, as it is such a good dual-purpose bird and matures quickly.

LEFT: A very proud Pekin cock.

Houdan – An old French breed that produces a fine carcass and about 200 large white eggs per year. They are very calm and easy to handle.

Barnvelder – Originally from Holland, these produce lovely dark eggs (approximately 180 a year). They are stunning birds, now kept mainly for eggs and breeding, but they produce a good-size carcass. They are a very hardy breed and friendly as well.

Brahma – A large breed with a gorgeous, docile nature. Their egg production is approximately 140 per year, but the eggs are a good size. They produce a large carcass, although they are rather slow to mature.

Dorking – these birds produce great meat and eggs (approximately 140 eggs a year). One of the oldest British breeds, Dorkings are hardy and friendly, but very active, so require plenty of space.

Faverolle – A French breed, these are really lovely, comical birds. They are quiet and friendly and rather affectionate (I find them difficult to eat because of this!). They thrive in a run and are not good flyers, so fencing doesn't have to be high. They lay approximately 160 eggs per year and make a good-sized carcass.

Orpington – These birds come in an array of colours. They lay 150–180 eggs a year and give a large carcass. They are very calm and easy to handle. These days, most are used as show hens.

Pekin – A small bantam breed, ideal if space is an issue. They are very popular as they are extremely friendly. Their eggs are small, but they lay around 120–160 a year. They also make wonderful broodies for rearing (see page 71).

Sussex – One of the oldest breeds in existence today. They lay 180–260 eggs per year, and give a good carcass, making them very popular birds to keep. They are friendly and happy to range freely or live in a run. They are not good flyers, so fencing does not have to be high.

Vorwerk – Originally developed in Germany, these are very attractive, alert and active birds, producing about 170 eggs a year. They are medium-sized and my sister has produced some lovely meals from Vorwerks, although I think they're too attractive to eat! They make a wonderful addition to a laying flock.

Swedish Flower Hen – Great dual-purpose birds, which lay approximately 200 cream-coloured eggs a year and produce a good, quick-maturing carcass, making them more cost-effective than some other breeds. They are very hardy, extremely inquisitive and friendly – not to mention beautiful.

Transylvanian Naked Neck: you either love these birds or hate them. They actually have half the number of feathers present on other birds, making them quicker to pluck! They are really hardy and produce a lot of eggs, about 200 a year, even in the colder months. The carcass they produce is superb.

The age at which the breeds listed above will start laying can depend on when the birds were hatched. Usually chickens reach this stage, known as 'point of lay' between 16 and 21 weeks of age. However, if they reach this stage in mid-winter, when the weather is extremely cold and the days short, they might not actually start laying until the spring. Feed and the environment are also factors. Birds can stop laying for a lot of reasons, including the weather, moulting, broodiness, illness or being moved. Generally, birds will lay for a good 5–7 years, but the quantity of eggs they lay will gradually decrease as they age. The age at which birds are ready to eat also varies. I tend to favour gauging when birds are ready by feeling them – skinny birds won't give you a good meal!

ABOVE LEFT: An inquisitive Faverolle hen. ABOVE RIGHT: A Frizzled Pekin Bantam and Japanese Booted Bantam crosses going to bed. OPPOSITE: Moveable breeding pens.

housing

The biggest threat to poultry is predators, namely foxes, wandering dogs and, occasionally, badgers. Fox-proofing your chickens is imperative, otherwise your chicken pen will just be a takeaway haven for your nearest fox! If you have lots of space and intend to move your run around, you can't beat electric fencing – it's relatively cheap, easy to use and works well, as long as it is set up and maintained correctly (see page 22).

You can buy huge, galvanised walk-in runs, which are easily moved by two people; these are very good as they have a top, too, which prevents wild birds getting in. Small, moveable arks with a run attached are also a very good option; go for one on wheels so you can move it daily without needing assistance. Using these runs gives you peace of mind that your girls are safe.

To keep predators out, you will need to put a skirt of wire about 25cm wide around the run; use tent pegs to fasten it down. It takes a few minutes to unpeg when you need to move the run, but it stops predators digging in underneath it. Some people prefer to wire the bottom of the inside of the run rather than making this skirt around the outside. I find this totally impractical, as chicken poo sticks to the wire, making cleaning a nightmare. It is also unpleasant for the birds to walk and scratch on.

Your chickens' outdoor space should include a sheltered area to enable them to get out of the sun or rain. This could be a small tarpaulin stretched over some poles, or an old table works well, plus you can place food under it, which is a bonus. Provide perches for your chickens – in the winter months, when the ground is frozen, they will appreciate being off the ground. Branches can be used, as can logs either placed on the ground or hung up. Make their environment stimulating and enjoyable: hang bunches of dock leaves or dandelions and provide a dust bath. This is a dry container of earth or sand for the birds to bathe in – an essential part of their daily routine. Bathing in the dust cleans their feathers, helping to remove and smother any unwanted mites.

A good tip is to add diatomaceous earth (see Glossary, page 220) to it regularly, which will kill any mites.

If you are keeping fast-growing meat birds, you will find that they do not perch, but do enjoy free ranging. Therefore I do not put any perches in with my meat birds, nor do I hang bunches up too high, as they are not as nimble as pure breeds or layers.

As well as a run, hens need a solid, safe house. They should be locked up in it at dusk, but they need access to it during the day, too, as they will lay their eggs in it and shelter from the weather. There is a huge array of hen housing on the market, so your choice will depend on what you are raising your girls for and how many you are keeping.

Housing should be easy to clean and dismantle – many modern hen houses can be completely dismantled with ease, making the eradication of red mite much simpler (see page 74). Never choose a coop that has a felt roof, as the material will harbour red mite, which are then impossible to get rid of. If you are buying second-hand coops, make sure that you disinfect them well and treat them for red mite just in case. Wooden houses are my preference, as I find them aesthetically pleasing. When buying them, make sure that the locks and hinges are robust and of good quality, and that the wood is thick enough to prevent predators getting in – predators have been known to chew their way through thin wood or weak catches. Thick wood will also provide adequate insulation during the winter months. Pop holes (the small entrances your chickens will use to get in and out of their house) are normally around 30 x 30cm, although this varies for larger breeds like the Brahma.

If you provide perches within the house, they should be removable to make cleaning easier. Perches for most breeds should be 4–5 cm wide, although larger breeds will require slightly larger ones.

Nest boxes should be provided for all the girls. I like using plastic boxes as they can be easily removed and cleaned. The boxes need to be easily accessible so that you can collect eggs – a good rule of thumb is one nest box per three hens.

There should be enough ventilation holes to allow air to flow, but not so many that the girls are exposed to draughts. Never close the ventilation holes in the winter – chickens need fresh air to prevent lung problems. Ventilation is often overlooked and always results in sick chickens.

Meat birds have simpler requirements: a draught-proof, well-ventilated house is all that they need. They won't need nest boxes, and perches are best avoided.

It is very important not to have a house too big for the number of birds living there. In the summer months the size is not a problem, but in the cold winter months the birds will find it difficult to keep warm in too large a space. I find it helpful to put a large cardboard box on its side in the coop in my larger hen house – that way the birds can huddle together in a smaller area which will take less body heat to warm. During the colder months, my poultry live in winter runs – these are areas with a thick layer of wood chip on the ground to prevent it becoming sodden, and tarpaulins covering the top and one side to provide shelter from the elements. I place my winter runs close to my house to make my life easier – nobody wants to be trudging miles in the rain and mud!

Please remember chickens love to run around, scratch, flap and jump, so the more space you can give them, the happier they will be. Runs will quickly fill with faeces and grass will turn to mud if your birds are kept in too small an area, so giving them plenty of space will also cut down the amount of cleaning you will have to do, giving you more time to enjoy their wonderful antics.

Cleaning

Regular cleaning is essential, as is a weekly check for mites, rodents or signs of damp. During the winter months when snow is on the ground for prolonged periods, it is beneficial to 'deep litter' the chickens. To do this, instead of clearing the old bedding out, put fresh bedding on top of the old, and continue to do this until the weather breaks. Leaving the old bedding under the fresh produces heat, which will rise and keep the girls warm. Make sure you clean thoroughly when the weather breaks. This method is used by a lot of smallholders to keep their charges warmer.

CLOCKWISE FROM BOTTOM LEFT: An easy-to-move wooden ark; two Salmon Faverolles keen to get out through their pop hole (with a Silkie hen in the way!); a breeding pen of Buff Orpingtons – note the covered area for shelter.

feeding

What you are keeping your chickens for, and their age, will determine what is best to feed them. Therefore the information below is intended as a guide only – every smallholding and every animal is different, and weather conditions, location and quality of feed can all have an effect on what and how much they need to eat.

Feeding chickens is very easy these days as there is a huge selection of readymade food on the market, for all ages. Which one you choose is entirely up to you, but try to buy food that is as natural as possible and non–GM.

One thing all chickens need to have available all year round is mixed grit. Mixed grit is a mixture of oyster shell, which provides a source of calcium that helps laying hens produce strong eggshells, and flint grit, which helps grind food up in the bird's gizzard, helping to prevent blockages. This in turn keeps the digestive system working well. As it doesn't rot or attract vermin, it can be frequently scattered on the ground, although it can also be placed in a suitable container and replenished when needed.

As a guide, laying hens require chick crumb from hatched to 6–8 weeks, rearer's pellets from 6–8 weeks to 16 weeks, and layer's pellets from 16 weeks onwards. They will appreciate mixed corn or wheat in the afternoon as a scratch feed – just enough thrown on the ground for them to forage and clean up in half an hour.

I always have feed available to my girls as the amount they need varies. If the weather is freezing, they will require more feed in order to keep warm. In the spring, when there is an abundance of bugs to eat and the weather is warmer, they will eat less.

CLOCKWISE FROM BOTTOM LEFT: An afternoon treat of mixed corn will always be appreciated by your hens; birds eating from an outdoor galvanised feeder; three rather shy purebreed chicks.

THE SMALLHOLDER'S HANDBOOK

Chick crumb – chicken feed with a high protein content designed for very young chicks.

Grower's pellets (also called rearer's pellets) – readymade chicken feed that is suitable for growing chicks

Layer's pellets – readymade chicken feed that is suitable for chickens laying eggs.

Finisher's pellets – readymade chicken feed that contains all the proteins and nutrients needed to make your chickens ready for the table.

I find they are not overly greedy but will take what they need, so this approach works for me. However, overfeeding can result in fat hens, which can lead to problems with laying, so if you think your birds are overeating you might prefer to weigh their food. Refer to the manufacturer's guidelines for quantities, as they will vary.

Meat birds are slightly different. They require chick crumbs from hatch to 4 weeks, rearer's pellets from 4–7 weeks, and then finisher's pellets from 7 weeks to slaughter. I like finishing my meat birds on only corn for the last couple of weeks; it gives the meat a lovely taste.

You can give all your chickens greens. They love dandelions, dock leaves and nettles, and also relish blackberries, sunflower hearts and tomatoes. It is important to remember that, under Defra guidelines, in the UK it is illegal to feed your birds any scraps that have passed through your kitchen. You can, however, give them anything from your vegetable patch that is suitable – just make sure it hasn't been in your kitchen first!

Feed containers

The best way to feed your birds is in suspended, specially designed feeders. These prevent the girls scratching food out, which can cause waste and encourage vermin. If your hen house is long enough to house the feeder, that is perfect, as this will stop wild birds popping in for a free meal. There are treadle feeders available – these have a treadle that the birds have to stand on before they will dispense feed, the idea being that it is much harder for vermin to get to the feed this way. I can't personally say I have had great success with these, but some people swear by them. If your hen house isn't big enough to accommodate the feeder, making a small shelter for it to hang from and removing it every night is helpful.

Adding garlic to their water occasionally is a great tonic for all chickens – just peel and crush one clove and place it into the water to infuse. It is also said to be a good preventative against mites (see page 74), as apparently they don't like the smell.

ABOVE: Suspending the water stops mud and dirt being scratched in.

THE SMALLHOLDER'S HANDBOOK

Water

Water needs to be available all the time during the day – you will be surprised by how much chickens drink. You should provide fresh water daily. If you can suspend the container, this will prevent too much dirt being scratched into it; if you are unable to do this, raising it slightly by popping it onto a few bricks will work too. Bucket drinkers are great as they can be filled and transported by wheelbarrow if water is not available nearby. Long troughs are not good for chickens, as they tend to perch on the rim and poo in the water, which is not hygienic. As with any animal, feeders and drinkers should be regularly disinfected – I do mine once a fortnight, as a rule. I use a great disinfectant called Virkon S, but there are plenty available. Just follow the instructions on the packaging.

breeding

A quick note before you get started – if you intend to breed chickens, please be aware that at least half of the chicks you hatch will be cockerels. If you are raising them for meat this won't be an issue, as both sexes can be eaten and you'll be planning to slaughter them anyway, but if you are raising them for layers, you will need to be able to 'knock them on the head' as soon as you know the sex. If you go for a self-sexing breed like the Legbar (a lovely breed that lays beautiful blue–green eggs, which can add real interest to your egg basket), you will be able to sex the chicks at a day old (see page 73 for more).

Remember, you need to have sufficient housing for your chicks; they don't stay small for long!

Cockerels

I keep my breeding birds completely separate from all my other birds and, as a rule, I keep one cockerel to four hens. An amorous cockerel can cause some terrible injuries to hens during spring, so you need

ABOVE: My sister's Rhode Island Red cockerel.

to file his spurs (the horny growth on the rear of his legs) so they are blunt or they will rip the girls' sides as he mounts them.

When you purchase your cockerel, he needs to be a good, healthy specimen with good feet, bright, clear eyes and a friendly nature – there is nothing worse than a large, ill-mannered bird that attacks you every time you go into his pen. Be prepared for the noise – cockerels love to crow. Unless you are breeding purebred chickens, the cockerel doesn't have to be the same breed, but some common sense is required;

putting a very small Pekin cockerel with a large Brahma hen is not going to result in chicks. He just won't be able to do the deed – although he will try!

Timing

Cockerels tend to be less active during the winter months. I often separate my cockerels from my hens for a few months in the winter to give the girls a break. Spring is the best time to breed your chickens. By this time of year, the weather will be improving, the grass is lush and the chicks will grow well with the sun on their backs. When breeding, I recommend running a cockerel with his girls for a week before you try incubating the eggs, to make sure the eggs you choose are fertilised.

Incubating

It is not possible to tell if a chicken egg is fertilised and developing until incubation has begun – the embryo will not start developing until it is at the right temperature and in the right conditions. Once you have begun incubation, you can 'candle' your eggs (see opposite) on days 4–6 to see whether they are fertilised and developing correctly.

Using a broody

If you have a broody hen (see page 59) that wants to sit and hatch the chicks for you, all you really need to do is provide her with a separate house and a run to rear in. The eggs don't have to be her own if she's broody – they don't even need to be chicken eggs! I have used broody hens to hatch quails, ducks, geese and turkeys.

It is easier to sneak the eggs in under her at night. A large hen can incubate up to 12 eggs, but a smaller bantam will manage only six – she needs to be able to cover them all comfortably and keep them warm. She will need to have food and water close by and sometimes you will need to physically remove a very determined broody from the nest so she can eat, drink and defecate. Extra vigilance for mites is needed during this time, as broody chickens are sitting targets for them.

Artifical incubation

To incubate the eggs yourself, you will need an incubator and a rearing pen with a heat lamp.

Eggs need to be collected daily from the hen house. Choose clean eggs that are not cracked and do not have noticeably thin shells. Any obviously misshapen eggs should be discarded. Avoid washing or wiping the eggs to be hatched, as this will remove the protective coating, called the 'bloom', which protects the contents of the egg from bacteria. Instead, you can clean them with a special egg sanitiser – it is a good idea to do this before placing them in an incubator, as if any germs get into that moist, warm environment they will multiply.

Eggs can be collected and stored for up to 7 days before incubating – after this time, fertility will begin to decrease. While you are storing them, turn them once a day to prevent the membrane sticking to one side. Fertilised eggs will take 21 days to hatch.

If you are using an incubator, read the manufacturer's instructions and follow them carefully. Incubators need to be placed in a room with a constant temperature and away from direct sunlight, which will make the temperature rise. Disinfect your incubator before use. You should also turn it on and run it for 24 hours, checking humidity and temperature levels, before use.

If you have a self-turning incubator, you do not

Before a female chicken lays her first egg she is called a pullet. After that she is a hen.

need to turn your eggs, but otherwise you will have to turn them by hand 3–5 times a day. Mark the eggs with a cross so you know when they are being turned; try to make sure that every night they sit on a different side. At 18 days you need to stop turning your eggs so that the chicks can get into the right position for hatching.

For the first 17 days of incubation, the temperature should be 37.5°C and the humidity should be around 53 per cent. (These levels are from my own experience using my incubators, so always check your manufacturer's guidelines as they may vary.)

When the eggs have been in the incubator for around 6 days, you need to 'candle' them to check their fertility and health. It's important to candle them at this stage, as unfertilised eggs can explode and contaminate the incubator. Candling involves holding each incubated egg individually up to a light so you can view its contents. Special candling torches or lamps can be purchased, or you can make your own – place a torch inside a cardboard box with a small hole cut in it, and sit the egg on top of the hole so that the light shines into it. It is best to do your candling in a darkened room.

Eggs that are not fertilised will be clear and can be discarded; those that are fertilised will have a dark blob with veins coming out. Eggs that have a dark circle inside can also be discarded, as this means the egg has failed to develop correctly.

Candling can also help you monitor the humidity levels by checking the egg's air cell, which is the space at the broad end of the egg. If the air cell is too small, it means that humidity is too high, and if it is too large, it means the humidity is too low. To adjust the humidity level, you will need to either add water to your incubator or remove some – check your manufacturer's instructions.

I candle my eggs again at 14 days to check that everything is progressing as it should be – if all is well, the embryo will have grown considerably – and

then I leave them for the rest of their incubation.

The first sign of hatching is called pipping; this is when the chicks break through the membrane and make a small hole in the shell. You will be able to hear them chirping. This is a very exciting time in our house – if you speak to them, they will answer you! It can take a good 24 hours for the chicks to hatch after they have pipped. It is not advisable to help the chicks out if they seem to be struggling; there is usually a reason for them having difficulty. It could be a problem with the temperature or the humidity, or just that it wasn't meant to be. Losses depend on your experience in incubation and rearing. Keeping healthy breeding stock, I would expect to lose about two chicks for every 50 that hatch.

rearing

Rearing with a broody

If you have used a broody to hatch the eggs, she will take care of the chicks when they hatch – you just have to provide chick crumb (see page 65) and water. Provide the water in a shallow dish with pebbles in, which prevents the chicks drowning.

Make sure the chicks are at least 8 weeks old before you introduce them to your other chickens – and observe them closely, as they can be attacked. Most of the time the mother will look after them, but sometimes they are relieved when their charges have fled the nest (aren't we all!) and will ignore them, so it's best to keep your eye on them to make sure all is well.

Rearing chicks yourself

You should wait for most of the eggs to hatch before removing chicks from the incubator, as lifting the lid too often at this point will affect the humidity. Most eggs should hatch within 24 hours. As the chicks are hatching, the yolk sac is absorbed through the navel – this will nourish the chick for 24 hours after

hatching, so don't worry about leaving them in the incubator while they dry off. Once the chicks have hatched and dried off in the incubator they should be moved carefully into their rearing box.

If you have chosen to buy day-old chicks rather than breeding and hatching them yourself, you can pick up the rearing guidelines at this stage.

Keeping your birds clean and dry is imperative with rearing chicks, as dirty, damp bedding can cause illness and with young birds this can be fatal. I use large plastic boxes, as they are draught-proof and very easy to clean. Line the bottom of the box with a layer of newspaper and, for the first week, top this with a layer of kitchen roll, the surface of which has more grip. This prevents the chicks from slipping, which can cause splayed legs.

The chicks need to be kept warm; this can be done by suspending a heat lamp above the box. It must be at least high enough that the chicks cannot touch the bulb, but you will have to adjust its height to achieve the right temperature. You will know when your chicks are at the right temperature, as they will happily run around, using the whole box. If they are too cold, they will huddle noisily under the lamp – this means you need to lower it, to bring the source of warmth closer to them. If they are too hot, they will disperse around the edge of the box – in this case, simply raise the lamp.

You are aiming to harden the chicks up by about week 4–5, but this will depend on the weather and time of year. To harden them up, raise the heat lamp gradually over this period. Observe your chicks, as they will let you know if they are happy or not. For the fourth and fifth week, turn the heat lamp off during the day and back on at night. After the fifth week, you can stop the heat completely.

Chicks will need chick crumb available to them

TOP: Rearing box with a selection of pure breed chicks.
BOTTOM: Pekin chicks enjoying the grass.

THE SMALLHOLDER'S HANDBOOK

how to sex a chick

Sexing chicks is difficult unless they are an auto-sexing breed (some breeds have distinctive characteristics or colouring unique to each sex). Your breeder should be able to tell you if this is the case. If your birds are not an auto-sexing breed, you could try vent sexing. This takes a lot of practice. It involves squeezing the faeces out of the chick, which will open up the vent slightly and reveal a slight 'bump' – girls have smaller bumps than the boys! It does take a lot of experience to get it right, so I'd recommend you simply wait until the chicks are 6–8 weeks old. At this age, combs and wattles will be bigger in the boys. They also tend to have bigger legs and feet and longer tails. Behavioural differences will also begin to show – if you observe them, you will notice the males sparring and strutting their stuff. I would recommend putting leg rings on or otherwise marking the ones you think are male for your first few hatches. You'll learn quickly and become more confident about sexing. And remember – they may not lay, but the boys do make lovely dinners!

as soon as they are dry and running around. Add a small amount of flint grit to aid their digestion. Do not add oyster shell for extra calcium to their diet at this age, as it can cause development problems and can also damage their kidneys. You can add small amounts of grass to their feed, but this needs to be finely chopped to prevent pasting (when droppings get stuck to the chick's bottom).

At approximately 6 weeks old, chicks should be out in their own coop. Move the coop regularly and protect them from the elements as you would adult hens. They should then be fed grower's pellets (see page 67) up until they are 16 weeks old. When changing their feed, do it gradually, mixing half chick crumb to half grower's pellets for a while.

Remember, when your birds are kept outside, you need to worm them (see page 74).

daily care

Your daily routine with your girls will be the same throughout the year. The only changes will be the time you lock them up and let them out, depending on the season.

Once you have unlocked your chickens in the morning, check their feed and water and top them up if needed. Take time to observe them for a short while – not only is this enjoyable, it will also ensure they are comfortable around you and give you the opportunity to check they are all well. Cast your eye around the perimeter fence to check no predators have been around and caused any damage overnight. Egg collection can be done now, but I find my girls tend to eat, drink, scratch around and stretch for a short while before getting down to the business of egg laying, so you may find it's best to do it later.

In the afternoon, I always go round with some corn that I throw into the run as a scratch feed. This is a good way to tame your girls, as they associate you with treats. They are not silly animals and quickly learn. An afternoon scratch feed, particularly in the winter months, enables the girls to get all the nutrients they need and go to bed full. Scratching around is also a natural behaviour for chickens that they really enjoy, and happy hens are productive hens.

When it begins to get dark, you need to lock your girls up for the night, making sure they are safe from predators.

health

Below are some common health problems in chickens.

External parasites

Red mite – This is a very common problem when keeping poultry. It is usually brought in by wild birds. Treatment can involve chemical sprays containing permethrin, but natural methods involve using diatomaceous earth powder (see page 220) regularly in the poultry house and on the birds. Smoke bombs can be bought online to fumigate the hen house if you have an infestation. As mentioned previously, garlic in the water not only provides the chickens with a health boost, it is said to prevent mites as they do not like the smell on birds. Eucalyptus oil sprayed lightly over clean bedding is also said to deter them. In my experience, you need to use a combination of treatments and use them properly in order to eradicate red mite. If left untreated, it can kill.

Northern fowl mite – This mite spends its entire life eating and breeding on the chicken. It can cause a lot of damage in a very short space of time. It is more often than not brought in by wild birds or on

birds that have not been checked properly when introduced to the flock. Signs to look for are dirty, greasy-looking feathers, especially around the vent area. In severe cases, dark scabs can be seen on the chicken's skin. Treatment is the same as for red mite. I have found that rubbing petroleum jelly onto the scabs helps after treatment.

Scaly leg mite – These tiny mites live on the bird's legs. They burrow in under the skin, causing the scales to raise and crust. They spend their entire life on the bird, and cause immense irritation and discomfort. Treatment needs to be carried out methodically and thoroughly. It involves washing the chicken's legs and treating them with appropriate sprays. I favour using surgical spirit on the legs regularly and then smothering them in petroleum jelly – this is an old-fashioned remedy, but it has always worked well for me.

Internal parasites

There are several worms that can infect chickens. Most can be controlled effectively by providing well-rotated, dry ground. You can worm your chickens regularly with a natural wormer. Verm-X is a great brand and, when used correctly, works very well. I use it on all my animals in combination with land rotation. There are chemical wormers available, but I am not in favour of using them regularly as this may lead to worms becoming immune to treatments. Land management and natural products are, I feel, by far the best option, unless you have a problem that is persistent. Before you start routinely dosing your charges, talk to your vet about other options.

Other conditions

Mycoplasma gallisepticum – Commonly known as 'myco' in the chicken world, this is a very common problem that a lot of poultry keepers experience.

ABOVE RIGHT: **Healthy legs and feet.** ABOVE LEFT: **The correct way to hold a chicken.**

Wild birds carry the disease and can infect free–range flocks. Stress, caused by things like moving your chickens, adding new chickens to a group or sudden changes in the weather can all be factors. Signs to look for include runny, 'bubbly' eyes, nasal discharge, coughing, sneezing and, in severe cases, swollen eyes. Treatment is usually a broad–spectrum antibiotic prescribed by your vet.

Infectious bronchitis – Otherwise known as IB, this has very similar symptoms to mycoplasma, but will infect your whole flock within a few days. If not treated, it will affect the nervous system and the chickens will develop droopy wings and a twisted neck. Most hybrid chickens are vaccinated against IB. Birds that recover are immune from getting it again, but become carriers. Treatment involves keeping the infected birds warm and looking out for any secondary infections that might need antibiotic treatment. Vitamin supplements added to their water helps. There is no known risk to humans from IB.

Prolapse – This is when part of the hen's oviduct protrudes from her vent. A hen with a prolapse is

easy to spot, as you will notice a large red swelling coming out of her vent. It usually occurs in older hens, but this is not always the case. An affected chicken needs to be quickly separated from the other birds as they will peck at it unmercifully, which can lead to her death. You will need to clean her back end with water and diluted iodine, then gently hang her upside down and try, with the help of gravity, to pop it back inside her. Keep her warm and quiet in a box of her own with food and water. If the prolapse reoccurs when she next lays, I feel that dispatching the chicken is the best option. If it does not reoccur, place her back with the other chickens only when all signs of blood have gone.

Moulting

Chickens usually moult once a year, at the end of the breeding season. They will lose their feathers and regrow new ones. Sometimes birds will drop almost all of their feathers very quickly, which can be rather shocking when you first experience it. Others can lose them in a specific pattern, starting from their head and neck, followed by their breast and body, and then the wing and tail feathers. It is a very stressful time for the birds and they may become lethargic. The process usually takes 3–4 weeks but can take up to 2 months. During this time, egg-laying ceases, although this occurs less frequently with hybrids. All chickens benefit from a poultry tonic to help them re-grow their feathers and lay eggs.

Wing clipping

Some chickens can be rather flighty, and you may find you have problems with chickens flying out of their enclosures. You can make them less nimble by clipping their wings. This sounds a little barbaric but it is actually completely pain free and temporary. The birds' wings have 10 flight feathers (also known

LEFT: The process of wing clipping, as described above.

as primary or quill feathers), which are the long feathers on the outer part of the wing. They also have secondary feathers on the inner part of the wing. The secondary feathers are there to keep the birds warm and must never be cut, but you can clip a bird's wings by cutting the flight feathers. Make sure you don't cut any lower than the tip of the other feathers (see pictures opposite). You need to clip only one of their wings; this unbalances them and makes them less agile. When done correctly with a sharp pair of scissors, it is completely painless, rather like cutting your nails. It is only a temporary measure and the wings will need to be reclipped when the feathers grow back.

slaughter

Dispatching your chickens can be a hard process, especially if you have grown fond of them, but it's important to take comfort in the fact that you've given them a full and happy life – and you can also be sure of giving them a quick and painless death.

Killing chickens or waterfowl should be done in a way that renders the bird immediately unconscious without any fear or pain, and quickly induces death before they recover consciousness. This can be achieved through the use of electrical stunning equipment, but most smallholders won't have this sort of thing, so the usual method is neck dislocation.

When done correctly, dislocating the chicken's neck will cause extensive damage to the brainstem and the bird will be instantly rendered unconscious. It's a quick and easy way of dispatching your birds, as long as you know what you are doing. It has to be done decisively, with a smooth, quick movement. If you hesitate or don't do it hard enough, you can cause the bird (and yourself) considerable distress. I would recommend you ask someone with experience to demonstrate the process to you, and then ask them to supervise your first attempt. This will reassure you and also ensure you develop the best possible technique.

First, catch your bird as calmly as possible and take it to a quiet place – make sure it is well out of sight of the other birds. Hold the legs in your left hand if you are right-handed, or right if you are left-handed. With your dominant hand, place the head in between your first and second finger and position your thumb under the beak, tilting the head slightly. With a very firm downward action, pull the neck and bring the head backwards. You should feel a 'pop' as the neck breaks – when you hear this, the job is done. The chicken will flap and kick for a short while. This is perfectly normal – it's simply a reaction of the nervous system and does not mean the bird is still alive or in distress. However, if you do not pull down hard and firmly enough, you will end up stretching the neck without actually killing the bird, which will cause it a great deal of stress and pain. If you're going to do it, you mustn't do it half-heartedly. Pulling too hard is better than not pulling hard enough. The worst that can happen if you pull too hard is that the chicken's head will come off in your hand. Of course, this wouldn't be very pleasant for you, but the bird would be none the wiser.

For instructions on plucking and drawing the bird, see pages 130–131.

legal guidelines

These guidelines cover the laws on keeping chickens in the UK. If you are outside the UK, it is best to check your own government guidelines.

As already mentioned, if you have over 50 birds in total, you need to register with Defra. You do not require a CPH number and no movement licences are required to move your animals. Defra states that it is legal and acceptable to keep backyard chickens anywhere in the UK. However, you do need to check with your local council as they may have by-laws

selling eggs

In the UK, selling eggs from your gate is allowed, but you must not grade them into sizes or describe them as free-range or organic unless you are a certified organic producer. If you wish to sell your eggs to someone who is going to sell them in a farm shop, you must register with the regional Egg Marketing Inspector. When selling your eggs, you must not wash them, as they are porous and protected by the 'bloom'. This is a damp layer that, when dry, allows the egg to breathe, but stops bacteria entering the egg. Eggs need to be sold in boxes, with the 'best before' date on them (which is 4 weeks from the day they are laid). It is best not to sell eggs from hens running with cockerels. I find that selling eggs from my gate usually makes enough money to cover the hen's keep.

that prevent you from keeping chickens in certain towns and even particular properties. You should also check the deeds of your house, as it is not unknown for individual houses to have a clause preventing them from keeping 'livestock', or at least limiting it. If you are a tenant – whether private, council or housing association – you need to check with the appropriate person or organisation.

Gathering eggs for food

Eggs should be collected daily. If you keep your chickens' houses and nest boxes clean, the eggs will just need to be placed in boxes. If there is a little dirt on them, gently remove it with a dry sponge. For optimum freshness and food safety, eggs should be kept at constant temperature below 20°C.

THE SMALLHOLDER'S HANDBOOK

Cloudiness of raw egg white indicates
an extremely fresh egg.

turkeys

You either love the appearance of these birds or you don't, but the vast majority of people will agree that they are extremely tasty. They are great characters, being both inquisitive and fond of human company. I have a turkey named Doris who is 5 years old. Every day she follows me around, talking for treats and chasing off sparrows! She's a real friend.

Keeping turkeys requires good husbandry skills as young turkeys (known as 'poults') are not very hardy compared with chickens. However, if you rotate your land regularly, do not keep too many for your space and avoid damp areas, particularly in their house, you will minimise any problems dramatically. Turkeys and poultry do get along, but traditionally, they were always kept separate to minimise the risk of blackhead disease (a disease caused by a parasitic infection that usually affects the liver and can cause the bird's head to become discoloured and blue). To try and reduce the risk of blackhead disease, I rear my turkey poults until they are about 10 weeks old away from my poultry and on land that has not had any poultry on it for a few months. After this, I feel that their immunity has been sufficiently built up, and they can be kept together. This works well for me.

Turkeys are also excellent 'guard dogs', great at raising the alarm when predators are around.

RIGHT: My old friend Doris, a Buff Turkey, displaying for the camera.

choosing a breed

There are many different breeds of turkey, from traditional breeds, such as the ones listed below, to commercial strains. I find that the varieties listed below do very well in free-range systems, produce fantastic meat and have lovely personalities.

Norfolk Black – Also known as the Spanish Black, these are one of the oldest turkey breeds in the UK and are considered rare. As their name suggests, they have dark plumage. Their meat is delicious.

Bronze – Named for the bronze-like sheen of their plumage, which is accented with shades of copper and blueish green. They are probably one of the most popular and well-known turkey breeds.

Buff – Pale birds with a cinnamon or red-brown plumage, these are smaller than some other breeds. They are quite rare these days, but Doris, who I mentioned earlier, is a Buff, and living proof of their friendly nature. I love Buff turkeys and would recommend them to anyone starting out. They are loving and easy to keep – that said, most turkeys are friendly.

Narragansett – These calm, friendly birds have black, grey, beige and white feathers and produce a good-sized carcass – but they are a rare breed.

Hen = female turkey
Poult = baby turkey
Stag/tom = male turkey

Bourbon Red – Named for their striking reddish brown plumage, these birds have a white band on their tail and beautiful white feathers at the tips of their wings.

Slate – These birds have slate-grey plumage, which is sometimes almost blue. They are known for their delightful nature and beautiful meat, but are quite rare.

Crollwitzer – These rather small turkeys have striking white and black plumage, which looks particularly impressive when they are displaying.

LEFT: A Norfolk Black turkey poult.
BELOW: A Bourbon Red turkey displaying.

housing

Housing turkeys is quite simple – a small shed (about 2.4 x 1.8m) can house up to six turkeys. It needs to be well ventilated, draught–free and dry. As with chickens, perches are needed. I use branches that I change as the turkeys' feet grow – they should be changed to allow proper grip. When a turkey perches, his toes should not touch each other under the branch. A gap of about 2cm is about right.

I don't use nest boxes for my turkeys; my breeding birds will make their own nest on the floor out of straw that I use to cover the floor – some of them even like to sleep on top of a bale. Any birds kept for Christmas will be gone before they lay.

When they're outside, turkeys need to be on dry, well–drained soil as they do not thrive in muddy conditions. Like all animals, they need shelter from the elements. I use corrugated bitumen supported on posts, as I have found the flapping of a tarpaulin in the wind scares them.

Electric fencing works very well at keeping predators out, but if the enclosure isn't big enough the turkeys will easily find a way to escape. Turkeys are great fliers and, if they haven't got enough space to flap and run around, they will certainly think the grass is greener on the other side! The more space you can give them, the happier they will be. However, as they fatten up they do become less nimble.

When it comes to winter, you should take the same steps as you do with chickens (see page 65) – although most turkeys will be eaten by then!

Cleaning

I clean my turkey house out weekly and follow the same routines as I do with my chickens, such as checking for mites and worms (see page 65).

locking up at night

Turkeys need locking up at night to protect them from predators. However, if you are late, as I was once, you may discover that they have decided to roost – in very high places! Even though they were settled right on top of their shed roof by the time I got there, I still wanted them locked up. My husband said that they would be fine, which I am sure they would have been during the night, but the problem would have been when they came down too early in the morning to a waiting fox! So it was ladders up and head torches on, and a very grumpy husband was made to help me get them down! His patience wore thin when the last one, which was just out of reach, refused to budge – so he gave it a gentle nudge with a broom. It flew, panic-stricken, straight at me, knocking me off the ladder. I landed on the floor with the turkey on my head! It goes without saying that I'm not late locking up the turkeys anymore.

RIGHT: Turkeys and poultry get along well and can happily range in the same area. Some precautions do need to be taken to prevent disease, however (see page 80).

feeding

Turkeys need a high–protein feed, so using feed specifically designed for turkeys is advantageous. You can buy turkey starter crumbs, which they can be fed from hatched to 5 weeks, followed by turkey grower's/rearer's pellets. If the birds are for the table, after 12–16 weeks you should move them on to finisher's pellets. They also enjoy maize and mixed corn. As with chickens, grit should always be available to help their digestion.

I feed my turkeys 'ad lib', meaning they have pellets available all the time. I do not feel they are greedy for them, and I find they take only as much as they need. I also feed them a scratch feed of corn in the afternoon.

ABOVE: Turkeys feeding from a raised container.

Feed containers

It is best if containers are suspended to prevent litter and dirt being scratched in. I use plastic feeders as they are lighter and easier to hang up in the turkeys' house. This helps to discourage wild birds from helping themselves to the feed and allows it to be locked up at night so rats are not tempted. You can also raise the feeder when required as the turkeys grow, making it easier and more comfortable for them to feed.

Water

The guidelines for water for turkeys are the same as those for chickens (see page 68). Never put their water inside the house. I like using galvanised bucket drinkers that are designed to sit on their side. They have a lip to prevent mud from being scratched into the water and I find my turkeys prefer them.

Carundle = the brightly coloured growths
on the turkey's throat area

THE SMALLHOLDER'S HANDBOOK

breeding

As I explained in the Chickens section, before you start breeding you need to make sure you have sufficient space for all your new arrivals, as they grow quickly.

Breeding turkeys is easy, unless you have hybrid/commercial strains, which can and do become too fat to mate naturally. If this is the case, it's easier to buy in fertilised eggs.

One male to 6–10 females (hens) is a good ratio for a breeding group, but this will depend on the breed – lighter breeds, like the Crollwitzer and Narragansett, do best on a ratio of about one male to 6 females.

Timing

The mating season starts in late January or early February. Turkeys will traditionally start laying eggs from February onwards, although my turkey, Doris, tends to favour June! Like other birds, they will produce young naturally when the weather conditions are right, so it is mostly likely to happen in the spring and early summer, when the days are longer and natural food and bugs are plentiful, giving their young the best chance of survival.

Incubating

As with chickens, you should choose clean, unbroken eggs that are not misshapen to incubate. You can clean them with a special egg sanitiser – it is a good idea to do this before placing them in an incubator, as if any germs get into that moist, warm environment they will multiply.

Using a broody

Female turkeys usually make great mothers; I have even used a broody turkey to hatch chickens before! They require a quiet, safe place to sit, and feed and water should be readily available. Treat them in the same way as you would a broody hen (see page 70); remove them from the nest twice daily to eat, drink and defecate, and dust them regularly for mites. Eggs will normally hatch on day 28, and then mum will take charge.

Artificial incubation

If you are using an incubator, read the manufacturer's instructions and follow them carefully. Incubators need to be placed in a room with a constant temperature, and away from direct sunlight, which could make the temperature rise. Disinfect your incubator before use, and turn it on and run it for 24 hours, checking humidity and temperature levels, before adding the eggs.

For the first 21 days, the temperature should be 37.5°C, with the humidity at around 55 per cent. After this, for the last week of their incubation, lower the temperature to 37°C and increase the humidity to 75 per cent. This is just a guide – it works for me, but check your incubator's instructions, as yours may be different. Keep records so you can see where you are going wrong or as a record for getting it right.

If you have a self-turning incubator, you do not need to turn your eggs, but if you don't you will have to turn them by hand 3–5 times a day. Mark the eggs with a cross so you know when they are being turned; try to make sure that every night they sit on a different side.

As with chicken eggs, you should candle turkey eggs to check that they are fertile and developing properly – see page 71 for more information.

Your turkey chicks will hatch at 28 days. Their hatching process is the same as for chickens (see page 71).

rearing

Turkey chicks should be reared in the same way as chickens (see pages 71–73) – so if they have a broody mother, she can rear them, and if not, you will need to rear the chicks in a rearing box with a heat lamp.

You need to provide turkey starter ration for your turkey chicks for the first 5 weeks. This has a higher protein content than chick crumbs. After this, you can move them on to grower's pellets and grit.

I aim to have my turkeys away from the heat lamps and outside in small pens at about 6 weeks, with the aim to have them out properly at 10 weeks. As with any young, this is very dependent on the weather.

When handling your birds, be calm and move slowly to avoid panicking them. If one bird gets panicked, they will all follow and chaos will reign, causing birds to bruise and injure themselves. In my experience, poults seem to have a knack of dropping down dead for no reason. Do not be put off or get too down about it – it just seems to happen with turkeys!

Daily care

The daily care of your turkeys is exactly the same as with chickens – see page 73 for your daily routine.

health

The main health problems with turkeys are blackhead (which I mentioned on page 78) and coccidiosis, which are caused by inadequate management of pasture rotation and dirty bedding. Keep turkeys on dry bedding, and never let it get damp. Both problems are caused by protozoans that attack the bird's digestive system and will need veterinary help to be diagnosed and treated properly with the appropriate medication. Symptoms of coccidiosis include lethargy, drooping wings, bloody diarrhoea and having a hunched appearance.

Worming is required regularly – I use Verm–X, which, if used correctly, is very effective. If you would rather use chemicals, Flubenvet is very good. Ask your vet to help plan a worming regime that suits your livestock, you and your land. External parasites that affect turkeys are the same as those that affect chickens and should be treated in the same way (see page 74).

slaughter

When dispatching turkeys, I find the best method is neck dislocation using a broom handle, as they are far too big to hold with one hand as you would a chicken. Calmly catch your bird and hold it upside down until it stops flapping. I always find that the birds I have reared know me and trust me so don't tend to flap for long. Once the bird has calmed down, let the head lie on the floor whilst you hold the legs firmly. The top of the head should be facing up and the beak should be pointing away from you. The broom handle (with no broom attached) should be placed on top of the base of the skull/top of the neck. You then need to place your feet on the broom handle, one on either side of the head, to securely hold the head still. Then pull upwards on the feet in one swift motion to dislocate the neck. This method is easier if you have someone there to help. You do need to be strong but, when done correctly, this will kill the bird quickly and humanely.

For instructions on plucking and drawing the bird, see page 130–131.

LEFT: Young Norfolk Black turkey poults exploring their pen.

guinea fowl

Originating from Africa, guinea fowl are (from the neck down, at least) stunning birds. They have a beautiful, plump body covered with gorgeous feathers – topped off with a comically tiny head. They are very hardy birds and good fliers, and they will happily roost in trees. Their eyesight is excellent and they devour creepy crawlies, so if you have a problem with slugs, beetles and weevils they will make quick work of getting rid of them. Like turkeys, guinea fowl make extremely good 'guard dogs', but may make you unpopular with your neighbours; they are truly noisy birds.

In my experience, they are not a bird to be tamed – at least, I have never managed it. They are busy, slightly neurotic things. My sister was adamant she was going to raise them and that she could tame them. Not one to argue with my big sister (she's always right), I just waited. After a few months the expected call came: 'I've had enough. They're noisy, they don't love me and they run around all day making a racket; they're in the freezer!'

Guinea fowl taste divine and you can also eat their eggs. They are very easy birds to rear, so if you have the space (and no close neighbours) I recommend you give them a try. They come in several colours – Pearl (grey with tiny white spots on, which are my favourite), White, Lavender, Pied, and Mulberry.

the birds and the bees…

It is not advisable to keep guinea fowl if you have bees. I once watched a couple of guinea fowl at a friend's; they just stood by the beehive and as the bees came out the birds snapped them up with relish.

RIGHT: Pearl Guinea Fowl sharing a pen with a Pied Guinea Fowl (white breast).

choosing a variety

All varieties of guinea fowl tend to start laying at around 25–28 weeks of age and lay an average of 150 eggs a year. The main difference between varieties is in their plumage.

Pearl – This is the most common variety. It has dark purple/grey feathers covered with tiny white spots (pearls) – a really stunning bird.

White – A pure white bird. I had a couple once and at night when they roosted in the trees they looked like ghosts.

Lavender – This variety is a light dove grey colour.

Mulberry – This variety has a purple body with a buff head.

Pied – These lovely birds have white chest feathers and sometimes a few more on the back area. Pied guinea fowl can be of various colours.

There are many other colour variations in America – you can also get Chocolate, Fauve and Silver-winged, to name but a few.

BELOW: **Two Pearl and one White guinea fowl.**
OPPOSITE: **Guinea Fowl checking out their electric fence.**

feeding

Good organic or free-range chicken pellets are great for guinea fowl; try to avoid cheap commercial feed, as this can be toxic for them. Guinea fowl tend to get a large proportion of their food from free ranging. They love bugs and will also eat mice and even small rats. They do eat plants, but are happiest hunting for bugs. If you are keeping only a few guinea fowl as 'pets', wild bird food is suitable for them, but grit is also needed. Feeding baby guinea fowl (keets) is easy; use chick crumb for the first few weeks before mixing in an adult ration.

As with chickens, water needs to be available to guinea fowl at all times. Provide them with fresh water daily and place it in a container that won't get dirt scratched into it.

housing

I only ever keep a few guinea fowl, and have never had to house them, as they happily roost in an old oak tree. When the weather takes a turn for the worse, they have the sense to come into the barn. That said, predators will take guinea fowl occasionally. Do make sure they have adequate protection (at least until they are able to fly). Before you free range your guinea fowl, enclose them in a barn or house for a few weeks so they become accustomed to home. If you prefer, you can keep guinea fowl in runs, in the same way as chickens (see page 63).

Like chickens, guinea fowl like a dust bath (a dry container of earth or sand for the birds to bathe in), which cleans their feathers and gets rid of mites, so make sure you provide one.

If you wish to keep guinea fowl on a larger scale, barns, large sheds or poultry houses can be used. As with all birds, ventilation is very important, as is a dry bed, good food and clean, fresh water.

breeding

Keeping a group of four hens to one male is ideal, although in the wild they tend to breed in pairs. It can be difficult to tell the sexes apart, although males tend to have bigger helmets and wattles. The easiest way to sex is by the noise they make. Females can make a two-tone call, but males have only a single call. This is apparent at about 8 weeks of age.

Incubation

Guinea fowl start to lay in the spring and tend to go off and find a quiet place to lay a clutch – under hedges is common. The incubation time is 26–28 days. Broody hens and turkeys can be used to hatch the eggs if you prefer, but guinea hens will incubate their own eggs – they just can't free range at this time. You will need to provide the female with an adequate house and run to keep her safe from predators while she sits and hatches them.

Artificial incubation

If you prefer, you can use an incubator rather than having a female hatch the eggs. Fresh, clean eggs should be used. You can clean them with a special egg sanitiser – it is a good idea to do this before placing them in an incubator, as if any germs get into that moist, warm environment they will multiply. The optimum temperature and humidity for guinea fowl eggs is the same as turkeys (see page 87). Candling (see page 71) can be difficult, as the eggshells are very thick, but it can be done at around 10 days.

If you have a self-turning incubator, you do not need to turn your eggs, but if you don't, they will need turning by hand 3–5 times a day. Mark the eggs with a cross so you know when they are being turned; try to make sure that every night they sit on a different side.

rearing

Young keets are very pretty, not dissimilar to quails. Guinea fowl should be reared in the same way as chickens – so if you are rearing them for meat, use chick crumb from hatch to 4 weeks, grower's pellets from 4–7, and finishing pellets from 7 weeks to slaughter. If you're rearing them to lay and breed, give them chick crumb from hatched to 6–8 weeks, grower's pellets from 6–8 weeks to 16 weeks, and layer's pellets from 16 weeks onwards.

If guinea fowl are being reared for the table, they should be ready at 11–14 weeks old, but this does vary.

health

Guinea fowl are very hardy birds but can suffer from the same ailments as other poultry (see pages 74–75). On a small scale, with good food and care, you should have no problems. Worming regularly and treating for mites is advantageous. Placing mite powder in their dustbath is a good way to do this.

Daily care

If you are keeping your guinea fowl in pens, their daily care is exactly the same as for chickens (see page 73). If they are free-ranging, just make sure feed and water are available at all times. They appreciate a feed of corn in the afternoon.

slaughter

Guinea fowl can be dispatched using the same method as for chickens (see pages 77–78).

For instructions on plucking and drawing the bird, see pages 130–131.

RIGHT: Free-range Lavender Guinea Fowl.

Guinea fowl babies are called keets
Cock = adult male
Guinea hen = adult female

quails

Quails are often overlooked because of their size, but really they shouldn't be. They produce gorgeous, tasty eggs and fantastic meat that is high in protein and low in fat, as well as containing higher amounts of minerals and vitamins compared with broilers (chickens raised for meat).

Quails are essentially shy, ground–dwelling birds. That said, they are good–natured and can be tamed with calm, slow handling. If disturbed or startled, they have a tendency to break cover, rather like pheasants, flying straight up into the air. I have lost a few birds this way, never to be found.

With very little space required compared with most animals, they really do have a place on a smallholding.

RIGHT: Coturnix quails feeling safe and secure in their hutch.

quail eggs

Quail eggs are perfect in salads and make the perfect healthy snacks for children – boil, but don't peel them and let your children do the peeling themselves! I did this regularly when I had four children under the age of 5 – it always took them a while, which meant I could enjoy a cuppa in peace! Quail eggs are also fabulous for dinner parties and picnics and make exquisite scotch eggs. You can preserve the eggs in brine or pickle them; they look stunning with their shells left on.

choosing a breed

The best dual-purpose quails, good for both meat and eggs, and the ones I personally keep, are Coturnix. They are great layers (they start laying their exquisite eggs at around 5–6 weeks of age) and produce a fine carcass, big enough to eat at about 8–10 weeks.

Most other types of quail are too small to keep for meat and are kept mainly by hobbyists as they are extremely pretty.

housing

Some people use aviaries for their quails, but this is an expensive option. I prefer to house my quails in large rabbit hutches. I find 4 females and a male per hutch works well for me. I adapt the hutches by replacing the roof of the run area with a panel covered in nylon mesh. This prevents startled birds from injuring themselves when they fly straight upwards, and allows natural light in. The bed area stays roofed, although quails do tend to lay their eggs anywhere. I also fix sliding doors to block off the bed area; that way, you can usher birds into the other section while cleaning to prevent escapees, creating a much calmer experience for all involved. You cannot let quails free range at any time; they need to be kept in enclosed runs, as they will fly off and hide – and once hidden, they are almost impossible to find again.

Quails flourish best in a temperature of around 16–23°C, so over the winter I move their cages to a shed or barn with good ventilation. Hutches can be placed on pre-made shelves at waist height for ease of care.

To aid egg production, I provide artificial light during the winter months when they are indoors – for a small house a 25-watt bulb is adequate. Aim to give them 15–16 hours of light a day (natural and artificial combined).

feeding

Young quails can be fed on chick crumbs, which have a high protein content. Use coccidiostat-free crumbs if you can find them. At around 6 weeks (the bird's reproductive stage) move them on to adult rations. Use purpose-produced quails layer's pellets; these are smaller in size than other layer's pellets. As with other birds, I find that quails will eat only as much as they need, so I make sure there is food available to them all the time.

Grit should be available to quails all the time – I recommend you fill a D-cup bird feeder with grit and secure it to their cage door so they can get to it whenever they like. The grit needs to be suitable for quails – poultry grit is too coarse, but finer mixed grit can be obtained from most good pet stores. Grit helps to keep the bird's digestive system healthy and to ensure strong eggshells.

Quails also love greens, which they quickly shred with their sharp beaks. It keeps them active and helps alleviate boredom, which can lead to aggressive behaviour. Lettuce, dandelions and dock leaves are all popular with quails. Hang them in bundles to add more interest for the birds.

Cuttlefish bones will help keep their sharp beaks in good condition – just make sure they are firmly secured to the cage.

Fresh water should be available at all times. Small plastic chick drinkers are ideal for quails.

If you cannot buy quail layer's pellets locally or on the internet, try making your own. Mix one part chick crumb (coccidiostat-free) with one part millet and one part canary feed.

breeding

The key to successfully breeding quails is purchasing good breeding stock to start with. Make sure the birds are active and healthy, with no visual signs of ill health. Ideally, they should be unrelated to prevent breeding or birth defects. When I started out breeding quails, I bought two breeding quartets from different breeders, which enabled me to build up my own breeding programme. I now keep them in breeding groups (5 or 6 females to a male), which helps prevent the girls getting damaged by over-amorous males – they have sharp beaks that they use to hold onto the back of the female's neck whilst mating.

Quails breed pretty much all year round but need plenty of daylight each day for their fertility to be good, so they are more naturally fertile in the spring and summer months.

Incubation

Make sure the males have been running with the girls for at least 10 days before incubating the eggs – this ensures a good chance of fertilised eggs. The eggs will take around 17–18 days to hatch.

Using a broody

Generally, Coturnix quails don't go broody, but it does happen occasionally, usually when birds are kept in spacious outdoor aviaries, mimicking their natural environment. If the females don't turn broody, you can use broody chickens instead. I once had a Silkie hen hatch 20 quails – it was a wonderful sight to watch them trotting after her. Most people use incubators, however, as you can hatch many more eggs in a controlled environment.

Artificial incubation

Use fresh eggs, preferably no older than 7 days, and make sure you have turned them at least once a day. Store them blunt end up in a cool room and use only clean, undamaged eggs to minimise disease. I use an egg sanitiser – there are several available on the market, so follow the manufacturer's instructions – before placing them in an incubator, as if any germs get into that moist, warm environment they will multiply.

Leave eggs to dry naturally before placing in the incubator.

Incubators should be placed in a room with a constant temperature away from direct sunlight. As always, disinfect and then run the incubator for 24 hours before adding the eggs. For quails, the temperature of your incubator should be 37.5°C, reducing to 37°C at hatch, but check your own incubator's instructions.

Humidity should be around 45–50 per cent, increasing to around 75 per cent at hatch. Again this

BELOW: **Quail chicks feeding.**

varies with different incubators, so keep notes on your experiences and adjust accordingly. It may take a few hatches for you to be nicely in tune with your incubator.

Candling (see page 71) can be done at around 5–7 days. Fertilised eggs will have a developing embryo, seen as a reddish blob with veins coming out, but with the speckled eggs it can be very difficult to see because the speckles stop the light getting through, obscuring your vision. I tend to just let nature do its thing, as the incubation period is so short.

Eggs should be turned regularly while in the incubator – 4–5 times a day. I find having a self-turning incubator invaluable. Stop turning the eggs on day 14, to enable the chicks to get ready to hatch. Incubators should not be open during this period as the humidity level will be affected, which can limit the chicks' ability to get out of the eggs. Their hatching process will be very similar to that of chickens (see page 71).

rearing

If you have used a broody, leave the chicks with her for a week or two, then transfer them to a rearing box. If you have used an incubator, once all the chicks are hatched and dry, transfer them to their rearing box.

When rearing quail chicks, make sure your building is secure from rats. I raise my quail chicks in large plastic boxes with wood shavings on the bottom and a heat lamp suspended over it. For the first couple of days, I place kitchen roll on top of the shavings to prevent the chicks' legs from splaying, as kitchen roll gives more grip. Once the chicks are confidently walking around, the kitchen roll can be removed.

Food should be provided in chick feeders, which allow the chicks' heads to enter, but prevent the chicks from scratching their food everywhere. Small

how not to clean out quails

Keeping quails clean and dry is essential. As they are very small birds and extremely quick, cleaning should be done slowly and quietly. I once asked my son to clean them out for me; I was horrified to find him using a vacuum cleaner for the task! And, yes, some were sucked into the hoover. He thought it would be a good labour-saving idea. I do despair at the men in my house sometimes. Luckily, the chicks were removed quickly from the hoover bag unharmed, although slightly shocked. My son now runs all his 'good ideas' past me first.

chick drinkers are great for water; place small, clean pebbles in the rim for the first week to prevent drowning. Water needs to be available all the time.

You need to start hardening your chicks after about 3 weeks. This involves gradually raising the heat lamps every couple of days. Watch your chicks' behaviour – if they are gathered around the edges of the box they are too hot; if they are huddled in under the lamp they are too cold, so raise and lower the lamps accordingly. The weather outside has a huge effect on how long it takes to harden the chicks up. In summer it takes only a short while, while in the cooler months it can take longer. Once the birds are fully feathered, the heat lamp can be dispensed with. Keep them indoors for a week before popping them into their outdoor homes. They should be kept with their own age group whilst rearing. Once they are fully grown, they can be mixed with older birds.

As they mature, select the best ones for breeding and egg laying – the remainder should be kept to mature for the table. They will be ready at about 8–10 weeks.

sexing

Coturnix quails are relatively easy to sex from about 3 weeks of age. The boys have a rusty coloured chest and the girls have a speckled chest. I find it impossible to sex before this age. As they get older, you will notice that the boys' marking becomes more defined. At around 6 weeks, they reach sexual maturity and the boys start depositing 'foam balls' on the ground, which look rather like shaving foam. It is at this age you need to watch out for aggressive males, as they can inflict horrendous injuries on other birds. Removing badly behaved boys is beneficial for a harmonious flock – and it means you can enjoy them for dinner instead.

Daily care and health
The daily care that quails need and the health conditions that affect them are the same as for chickens, so see pages 73–77.

preparing for the table

Preparing quails for the table differs slightly from other poultry, as you are dealing with a much smaller bird.

Dispatch
Remove feed and water 6 hours before slaughter. Dispatch your bird humanely and out of sight of the other birds. The usual way is to sever the head in one quick movement; I use a very sharp pair of garden shears. If you are in the UK, I recommend referring to the Humane Slaughter Association website for guidance – elsewhere, please check your own country's guidelines to ensure your method of slaughter is humane.

Plucking and eviscerating
Once the quail has been dispatched, you need to pluck your carcass. This can be done dry or wet and it is covered in more detail on page 130.

When drawing the innards out of quails, I find it helpful to insert a small spoon into the vent opening and rotate it slowly to loosen the innards. You then need to gently draw the innards out of the enlarged vent opening.

The quick way
I prefer to prepare my quails in a much quicker fashion than other birds. Skip the plucking stage and instead snip the head off, then snip the legs off just below the feathering. Break the wings and then snip them off close to the body of the bird. Hold the body of the bird, breast side up, in your cupped hands. Using your thumbs, push down on the breast bone and pull it apart. The skin will split easily. You then need to peel the remainder of the skin off, leaving you with a skinless carcass. Now flip the bird over in your hand so that the spine is facing up. Using your shears, insert into the vent area and cut along the spine. Repeat this on the other side and pull the spine out along with the innards. Pull the remaining entrails out – these can be fed to your dog. Rinse the bird and place it in a bowl.

It takes me about 3–5 minutes to do this, which is much quicker than plucking. Remember an average person will need two quails per serving.

ducks

Ducks always attract people: village ponds, canals and rivers seem to be a magnet to people when ducks are present. There is something rather therapeutic about feeding ducks and watching them dabble and swim.

Keeping ducks is very simple, but I cannot emphasise enough how messy they are. Ducks need water and that leads to a muddy mess! That said, they have tasty meat and will provide you with fantastic eggs that are great for baking. They are also very good at clearing slugs. If you can tolerate the extra mud, they make a great addition to any smallholding.

RIGHT: A group of stunning Muscovy ducks. For more about this breed, see page 104.

choosing a breed

There are so many breeds of duck to choose from, from ornamental ducks to large meat ducks, so whatever space you have, there will be a duck to suit it. Do your research, speak to other people who keep them, consider the space available and be sure what you want to keep them for. Once you have this information, you can choose your breed and enjoy them.

Purebred ducks have their own characteristics that will vary from breed to breed, but there are also hybrids available that have been bred specifically for meat and/or eggs. Whatever breed you choose, the ducks you select should be in a healthy condition, alert and active with clear eyes. Their posture should be good, their eyes and nostrils should show no signs of discharge and their vent (bottom) should be clean. Ducks are normally clowns, so don't choose a quiet one that sits in the corner. Here are some of the most popular breeds.

Hen = adult female
Drake = adult male
Duckling = baby duck

Indian Runner – A truly comical breed and aptly named, as it runs everywhere. This is a very upright duck that likes to be with others. When in a group, these ducks will all run together, changing direction like a school of fish, which can be very entertaining to watch. They come in an abundance of colours and are flightless, which makes them easy to pen but susceptible to attacks from predators. They are very good layers, producing around 180–200 large eggs a year. They have a rather nervous disposition.

Cayuga – A large, stunning bird, with black feathers and a wonderful petrol-coloured sheen, which looks glorious on sunny days. It is a quiet, friendly breed that produces a good number of eggs – about 100–150 per year.

Muscovy – You either love or hate these birds. They have a distinctive red mark on their face, which some people dislike, but I find them very friendly. They are fantastic mothers and can be found in a variety of colours. They love to be out and about and mine spend a lot of time with the geese. They are very good flyers and enjoy perching, so they appreciate a few logs in their enclosure. When handling, be very cautious as they have strong, sharp claws. They produce 160–190 large white eggs per year and make a fantastic carcass.

CLOCKWISE FROM LEFT: A Mallard and a group of Call Ducks; a Call Duck (background) and White Campbell Duck (foreground); Muscovy Ducks.

Rouen – This is a huge duck that is beautiful to look at, its colour being similar to the wild mallard. The fact that is it slow-growing has led to its decline as a table bird; it is now mostly used as a show bird. It lays 140–180 eggs per year that vary in colour – they can be blue, green or white. Rouens are real head-turners and have a lovely nature, but they do have a tendency to be lazy, so make them walk for their food! This is particularly important if you want to breed from them, as fat, lazy ducks will be less fertile.

Silver Appleyard – These birds are really lovely and you can obtain large dual-purpose ones that are great for eggs, laying 200–250 per year, and meat. There is also a miniature version that is good for eggs, although the downside is smaller eggs and a smaller carcass. They have green mallard-like heads and silver-grey bodies. They are good mums and are easy to keep. Of all my ducks these are usually the first to start laying in the spring.

Pekin – A bird with more of an upright stance than other ducks, it originates from China and is a fast-growing meat breed. It has apricot or white plumage, a really cute face and produces mainly white eggs, laying about 200 per year. It's a real character to have around. This bird, like the Rouen, has a tendency to be lazy and become too fat, which will affect fertility.

Orpington – These are great birds to breed as a hobby. They are fantastic egg producers, laying about 150 per year, and the drakes make good table birds. They are friendly and hardy. Buff is the most popular colour but there are other colours around such as chocolate, blue, white and black, but they are rather difficult to find.

Saxony – Originally from Germany, this is another lovely dual-purpose bird that lays very well and makes a quality carcass. They are beautiful birds to have around and are easy to keep.

Aylesbury – Finding a nice Aylesbury is rather difficult, as it seems nowadays any white duck is called an Aylesbury. A true Aylesbury is pure white with a broad, long, flesh-coloured beak; a yellow beak is an indication of impurities in the breeding. There are an awful lot of commercial lookalikes out there! They are great table birds, fast-growing, hardy and easy to handle. They are not the best egg layers and because of their size can have fertility problems – their weight makes them less agile, which makes mounting females difficult. They are happier breeding in water, as this takes some of their weight and makes mating easier.

Call Duck – These ducks are so cute, but so noisy – they were originally bred to be used as decoys to 'call in' wild ducks by shooters. If you and your neighbours don't mind what can be, in the spring, constant quacks, they are great little characters to have around. A good Call Duck will have a lovely rounded head with a short, broad bill. Many people sell mixed ducks (when lots of different breeds have been bred together) as Call Ducks, so be careful. You can spot a mixed duck rather than a Call Duck as the mixed duck's beak will be much larger. Call Ducks are perfect for a small area and are good mums. They are very good layers, laying small white eggs. The amount of eggs varies hugely – some can lay about 80, although I have never had this many! Call ducks that have been breed for exhibition may only lay between 8-30 eggs per year. Of all the ducks I have kept, these are by far the friendliest; they really do make great companions and enjoy human company.

LEFT: White Call Ducks enjoying a drink (and the mud!)

housing

Duck housing is very simple. Ducks require no perches or nest boxes, and there is also no need for windows, as ducks do not use their houses during the day. However, they do need good ventilation. Flooring should be dry and solid, as they don't like wire or slats. Their housing also needs to be predator-proof, so your duck house should be made of wood that is of a decent thickness. Ideally, raise the house up about 20cm off the ground to prevent vermin from taking up residence underneath. You will need a ramp up to the house (ducks are not good jumpers). It will need rungs on the ramp so the ducks do not slip and it needs to be the same width as the opening.

If the house is positioned directly on the ground, wire the bottom outside and about 5cm around the outside to make sure nothing will chew through.

ABOVE: My duck house, with its small pond made from a large flexi bucket, is perfect for Call Ducks. **BELOW:** Herding ducks to lock them up for the night.

The houses need to be tall enough for the ducks to stand up in, so the height will vary depending on the breed. Ducks do not like pop holes; they are always in a rush to get out and, unlike chickens, they run out in a group, which can cause panic if the house does not have big enough doors through which to exit. Doors should be open all day in order to let air circulate in the house.

Where you position your duck house is very important if you want to reduce muddiness. The ideal position is on a slight slope on sandy ground; alternatively, surround the house with a thick layer of gravel, concrete or shingle for better drainage. In wet weather, ducks will make the ground a real muddy mess and then walk all this mess into their houses. A thick layer of straw makes ideal bedding and will need to be changed twice a week. Ducks mess an awful lot and their waste is very watery, which makes the bedding sodden very quickly.

Ducks love to free range, so an area cordoned off with electric fencing is perfect for them. Alternatively, you can have a wired run with a roof and skirt to protect them from predators. It will need to be big enough for a small pond and the ducks need to be able to flap their wings and run around.

Shelter should be provided to protect them from prevailing winds; this can be straw bales, windbreaks or bushes. When choosing a run, remember you have to be able to empty and refill the pond regularly, so it needs to be easily accessible.

ponds

All waterfowl require water to be happy and healthy. This can be a large pond, a stream, a child's paddling pool or even a large bucket. The most important thing is that the water needs to be clean. If it is stagnant with decaying matter in it, it will provide the perfect environment for germs to breed, which can in turn make your ducks ill, cause eye infections and leave their plumage looking mucky.

Children's paddling pools (the solid plastic ones) are ideal as they are cheap and relatively easy to empty. Dig a hole in the ground exactly the right size for your paddling pool, so that the top sits level with the ground, and surround the pool with a layer of gravel to stop the area around it becoming too muddy. Then all you need to do is provide a non-slip ramp for access and you will have happy ducks. Paddling pools can be easily emptied using buckets, and the old water can then be used to water the vegetable patch – perfect!

If you have room for a larger pond, you can try making it the traditional way. Dig out the ground to the desired shape and depth, add clay to the hole and stamp it down until there is a layer approximately 20–25cm thick. Next, place a layer of silt on the top and allow it to settle. Once settled, fill the pond with water.

However, pond liners are more commonly used; choosing a good-quality one is essential as the claws

A group of ducks is called a raft, a team or a paddling

of some ducks can damage the liner. Just dig a hole to the desired size and make it level. Remove any stones, as these will damage the liner. Line the hole with a layer of sand, then underlay, and then place the liner in the hole and gradually fill with water, folding the liner and arranging it following the manufacturer's instructions. When you are happy with the pond, line the edge of it with gravel to finish the look.

You can also buy a pre-built rigid liner. As with most things, the trick here is preparation. Digging to get the pond level is the key to avoiding a lot of unnecessary stress and frustration. If you are planning to have a permanent pond, you will again need to plan very carefully, thinking about drainage or the cost of a pump, as you will need to clean it occasionally.

Ducks do not need a huge pond. Most can manage with a large bucket of clean water into which they can submerge their heads and preen themselves. I prefer to give them a small pond so that they can have a splash – in my opinion this makes them much happier, and I love watching them while they are splashing about.

If you are lucky enough to have a lake or stream for your ducks, protect the banks with chicken wire secured with pegs (this stops the ducks dabbling around the edges and eroding the bank). Remember, ducks need to be able to get out of the pond as well as in, so placing a few rocks in and around the edge will help them to get out. Alternatively, place a slatted ramp for them to walk up.

Problems can occur when ducks splash too much water out, decreasing the level of water. This can lead to them having difficulty exiting the water, so keep an eye on your water levels.

feeding

Feeding ducks is very simple, as you can purchase special duck feed in pellet form, which they love.

They do very well on chicken layer's pellets and I find that feeding them the same diet as my chickens (layer's pellets in the morning and mixed corn or wheat in the afternoon) works very well. If you are rearing meat ducks, you can purchase pellets specifically for table birds. Ducklings need chick crumb for the first 4–6 weeks, then grower's and finally layer's pellets for laying ducks and finisher's pellets of corn for meat ducks. Feeding your breeding birds a good-quality breeder's ration is imperative for healthy offspring. It is also important to have plenty

THE SMALLHOLDER'S HANDBOOK

ABOVE: A Call Duck dabbling in the mud.
LEFT: A selection of Call Ducks.

of poultry grit available to aid their digestion.

Ducks filter their food in water through their bills. It is important to have their food near the water – if you watch ducks feed you will see that they will take some food and then have a drink before having more food. They are also great foragers and enjoy insects.

Occasionally it is good practice to add minerals and vitamins to their feed to prevent diseases. I tend to do this just before winter and again at the beginning of spring. Verm–X do a great Poultry Zest and Keep Well Tonic that is suitable for ducks.

Ducks love bread, but it should be given only as a real treat and in small quantities, as you really want them eating their proper feed that has all the goodness they need.

breeding

If you do not want to breed your ducks, you do not need a drake (male duck) as the females will lay eggs whether you have one or not. Ducks are often sold in threes (two females and a male) rather than larger groups, as the males are less in demand and so breeders are keen to get rid of them, but I think it is kinder on the girls to have more ducks, as the drakes are rather rough lovers and it's much easier on the girls if there are more of them. If you choose to start with ducklings, remember you will get lots of drakes.

Depending on the breed of duck you have chosen, one drake to four or five girls is a good ratio. If you have chosen a heavier breed, such as the Rouen, a ratio of one drake to two girls is better for fertility. Heavier breeds also require a pond to mate in because of their size.

Incubation

Many ducks, notably Call Ducks, Indian Runners and Muscovies, make fantastic mothers, but with certain breeds, like Rouen, using a broody hen or incubator is much more reliable. Eggs take 28 days to hatch, but some may hatch a couple of days on either side.

All eggs chosen for incubation should be clean, undamaged and fresh. You can clean them with a special egg sanitiser – it is a good idea to do this before placing them in an incubator, as if any germs get into that moist, warm environment they will multiply. Like chicken eggs, duck eggs can be stored before you set your incubator or broody, but fertility starts to drop off after about a week. Incubators should be disinfected and run for 24 hours before you add the eggs. Set it to the correct temperature and humidity – for ducks, this is approximately 37.5°C, with humidity at about 60 per cent, increasing to about 75 per cent for the last week before hatch. These are guidelines only – read the instructions for your incubator as they vary. Make sure your

Most ducks are monogamous for a breeding season.

incubator is set in a room away from direct sunlight and with a constant temperature, as this can affect your incubator's performance.

If you have a self-turning incubator, you do not need to turn your eggs, but if you don't you will have to turn them by hand 3–5 times a day. Mark the eggs with a cross so you know when they are being turned; try to make sure that every night they sit on a different side.

Candle eggs (see page 71) at about 10 days and dispose of any that are not fertilised – these will be clear. While candling, check that the humidity levels are correct by checking the air cell.

Hatching

Stop turning eggs about 5 days before they are due to hatch, so that the ducklings can position themselves ready to emerge. They can take 48 hours to hatch but, if the temperature and humidity have been correct, all should go well.

If a duckling fails to hatch successfully, there is usually a reason and I feel it's best not to interfere. The exception is Call Ducks – because of their small beaks, they sometimes have trouble making the initial breakthrough, so I do sometimes help them by making a small hole in the air sac end. Candle the egg (see page 69) and look for a safe place to make a hole – the safe area will appear lighter. This needs to be done very carefully as you do not want to harm the duckling. I use a small clean pair of tweezers.

My daughter loves hatching time and will often wait up all hours of the night to wait for the ducklings to emerge. She is convinced that ducklings believe the first thing they see when they hatch is their mother, and seeing her being followed everywhere by lots of them, I do believe it too! It is a really lovely sight that cannot fail to make you laugh.

rearing

Once hatched, ducklings need to be reared in the same way as chicks (page 71–73), with the exception of the water dish. Ducklings require a larger dish, although it should still be very shallow, with clean pebbles in so they do not drown. When they are a couple of weeks old, a new, clean paint tray is ideal as there is a ramp for them to use. Ducklings sometimes need to be tempted to eat and drink; you can do this by sprinkling a small amount of crumb in front of them and dipping their beaks in the water – they soon catch on and then there's no stopping them!

Once your ducklings have been weaned off the heat in the same way as chicks, they can go outside. A simple house with a completely enclosed run is adequate.

You will notice that ducklings that are hatched naturally by their mother will be ignored by her as she loses interest in them at about 6 weeks. Feed your ducklings on chick crumb for the first 5 weeks – adding finely chopped grass will keep their digestive system working well. From 5 weeks, grower's pellets should be used, then from 14 weeks switch to layer's pellets, or a finisher's ration or corn for meat birds. Grit should be available all the time from the first week onwards; flint grit is perfect for ducklings – oyster shell is not really needed until they are about 14 weeks old.

health

Ducks are hardy and, compared with chickens, have few health problems, provided they have access to clean water, dry beds and good feed. However, ducks are prone to lameness. If you see a duck limping, it is normally a strained ligament. Rest is required; place the duck in a box with feed and water so it can't move around and has to rest its leg. After several weeks it should right itself. You do need to check that the injury is not a break – this can be felt easily. If the duck's leg is broken, sadly dispatch is the only option. Leg problems can be avoided by having wide entrances to houses and non-slip ramps; ducks should also have adequate ramps in their ponds.

Here are some other conditions to look out for:

Botulism – This is a deadly condition caused by a poisonous toxin, and is down to stagnant, dirty water, usually in the warmer months. This is definitely due to bad husbandry skills and can easily be avoided by making sure water is clean and fresh. Birds affected by this will often throw their heads backwards and appear disorientated; ultimately it causes paralysis and is usually fatal. A vet should be contacted for advice immediately.

Worms – Worms can affect ducks, especially when they are free ranging in overused paddocks. As I've already mentioned, ducks will quickly turn grass to mud, so it is good practice to rotate land very regularly anyway, but doing so will also help to prevent worms. Use Verm-X wormer regularly as a preventative measure. Only use a chemical wormer if your birds are looking ill – ducks that are unwell will appear depressed and be less active. If possible, do a

worm count before administering any drugs. A worm count involves sending a small sample of dung to a laboratory, where it is examined to find out if worm eggs are present in it and, if so, how many.

Prolapse – Prolapse is much less common in ducks than it is in chickens (see pages 75–77). The vent will protrude and hang out. Sometimes, if caught early, it can be cleaned and re-inserted carefully. This is easily done if the bird is hanging upside down as gravity will help, but I would recommend you ask a vet or experienced friend for help if you have not done it before. If the problem continues or the vent fails to go back inside the bird, culling is the best option.

Eye problems – Ducks can suffer from runny eyes, usually caused by a bacterial infection, which is often down to inadequate clean water. Eyes will need to be swabbed with cotton wool and salted warm water twice a day, then treated with antibiotic cream or drops from your vet. Make sure you wash your hands after treatment, as ducks' eye infections can be passed onto you.

Runny eyes may also be caused by a foreign object in the eye, so check your birds' eyes carefully; grass seeds sometimes get caught in their eyes, but are easily removed.

If you ever notice several of your birds being ill with the same symptoms, you should always call a vet. Likewise, if a duck is unwell for more than a few days, it should always receive veterinary help.

preparing for the table

Ducks should be slaughtered in the same manner as chickens or turkeys, depending on the size of the bird and how strong you are (see pages 77–78 and 89).

For instructions on plucking and drawing the bird, see pages 130–131.

Eggs
Duck eggs can be gathered, eaten and sold at your gate in the same way as chickens' eggs (see page 78).

ABOVE LEFT: An assortment of happy ducks, including Aylesbury, Muscovy and Call Ducks.
BELOW LEFT: The simplest and safest way to hold a duck. If done correctly, the bird will stay calm.

My daughter has a real soft spot for ducks. She once had an Indian Runner called Miranda that followed her everywhere, even into the shower...

geese

Geese are a lovely sight on a smallholding, with their comical waddle and knowing eyes. They produce wonderful eggs that make yummy omelettes – and nothing beats a lovely roast goose! They make fantastic 'guard dogs', but they are very noisy, so if you have neighbours you really should check that they do not mind.

You need plenty of space for geese as they are grazers, so do make sure you have adequate land with good-quality pasture that is not overgrazed by other animals. I usually allow about half an acre (about 2000 sq m) for four geese, but I like my animals to have space and grass in abundance, so you may choose to use slightly less land. The land should also be rotated regularly to avoid a build-up of worms. They enjoy new grass over long, lanky grass. Mowing regularly will encourage new growth and new tips, which they love, and grazing with sheep or cattle works well. Geese love to keep themselves clean (although they make a considerable amount of mess!) so access to ponds is necessary.

I often hear people say that geese do not need fox-proof pens, as they will see the fox off. I disagree strongly with this, as predators can and will attack geese. Unless they have a large lake with an island to sleep on, geese should be locked up at night and be protected with electric fencing during the day. I have lost geese to foxes, so I am speaking from experience.

RIGHT: Embden Geese happily sharing space with some ducks.

choosing a breed

You really need to do your research as there are lots of breeds out there. Geese fall into three groups: light breeds, medium breeds and heavy breeds. Some are great for meat and some just for eggs, some as ornamental pets and others as lawnmowers! Here are a few to get you started.

Sebastopol – This is a very distinctive-looking light goose, known for its curled feathers. It is often called the 'pantomime goose'. It is a gorgeous-looking bird and a real head-turner. Sebastopols have a lovely temperament and I have never had any trouble with mine. The ganders are good to eat, but most are sold as pets and to show. They need a mud-free pen to keep their feathers clean, and protection from the elements is a must; their feathers do not sit close to the body, so heat will be lost at a greater rate than with flat-feathered geese. They make very good, attentive mothers.

Pomeranian – An ancient German breed that is very hardy. They are great layers, producing 60–80 eggs a season, and are good to eat. They are chatty, medium-sized geese that are social and enjoy greeting visitors noisily, which can be a bit of a downside when you have a gaggle (a group) – but perfect for raising the alarm for predators and intruders.

American Buff – A really docile heavy breed, these geese are calm and easy to keep. They make very good parents and rear their goslings well. They produce medium/large roasting birds that taste delicious – a really good first-time bird. They don't lay much, however – about 15–25 eggs a year.

Greylag – This goose is thought to be the ancestor of most domesticated geese, with the exception of the African Goose and the Chinese Goose, which are believed to descend from the wild swan. They are calm but very noisy birds, and are mainly kept for ornamental purposes, although you can eat them. They are not great layers as they tend to lay a clutch of 6–8 eggs and then sit on them resolutely to hatch.

RIGHT: A Greylag goose

Toulouse – This is my husband's favourite breed. I have to admit that this heavy bird, with its cuddly, dopey expression, will steal a piece of your heart! Originating near Toulouse in France, these geese produce a large carcass. Because of their placid, docile nature they can get bullied by other breeds, so they are best kept with their own kind. They don't tend to wander far, making them ideal for a smaller plot. They are reasonable layers (around 20–40 eggs a year) but don't make great parents, so incubation is probably best.

Embden – The most popular table birds around, heavy Embdens are also the tallest. They lay around 30 eggs per year. They can be extremely protective of each other and of their goslings in the spring, making them slightly more challenging to keep, so they are probably not the best breed for the beginner. We had a couple of surplus ganders one year that we reared for Christmas; they were nicknamed the 'bad lads', and with good reason! My Jack Russell, having been attacked by both birds, eventually gained both a huge respect for geese – and a bare patch on her bottom. So if you have small dogs, take note!

African – I love the friendly personalities of these heavy geese. They aren't great layers (30–40 eggs a year), but they do produce a lovely lean carcass.

LEFT: Embden Geese standing guard.
RIGHT: My African Goose and two Embden Geese walking their turf.

THE SMALLHOLDER'S HANDBOOK

ganders

A gander within a flock is a lovely sight. Ganders are fiercely protective of their wives and watching their social antics is very therapeutic. That said, ganders can be aggressive and they are very powerful birds. I have had a few nips and they really do hurt, so be very careful, particularly if you have small children. You really do need to be the boss with ganders and I find that if they go for you, standing your ground and, if necessary, grabbing their neck to unbalance them can show them that you will not tolerate bad behaviour. Don't run away squealing, as my daughter once did. The gander in question never forgot this and whenever he caught sight of her, he would chase her mercilessly – although very amusing to watch it was rather traumatic for her! If a gander becomes too aggressive to cope with, culling is really the only option.

housing

A small shed (measuring about 1.5 x 2m) is ideal for a few geese, but if you have more, you'll need a larger space. Whatever you use, ventilation is very important. I remove the windows and cover the hole securely with wire netting, and then drill holes in the opposite wall for ventilation. Linoleum that has been cut to size and placed slippery–side down will protect the floor from rotting, as their faeces can be rather watery. A good layer of straw is the perfect bedding, but weekly cleaning is a must.

Geese don't need perches or nest boxes, but a ramp is appreciated for easy access in and out of the house. Place the house on free–draining soil and, as with ducks, place the house on the highest piece of ground. As geese need to graze, electric fencing is the best option as you can move it about regularly in order to rotate your land. If you are lucky enough to have an orchard they will love this area, as they'll enjoy foraging the fallen fruit and the bugs it attracts.

Geese cope very well in winter and are not averse to tramping around even in fairly deep snow. Care does need to be taken, however, as predators can be particularly hungry at this time of the year and electric fences can be inadequate at keeping them out.

feeding

The main diet of a goose is pasture, supplemented morning and evening with wheat – I allow one small cup of wheat per bird. When the grass stops growing and the colder months draw in, more feed will be required. If you are breeding geese, it is good practice to feed them breeder's pellets through winter to early spring to ensure they get the correct minerals and vitamins to produce healthy offspring.

Water

Clean water must be available at all times. During the winter months, it might be necessary to break any ice and refresh a couple of times a day. Like ducks, geese need ponds (see pages 109–110).

LEFT: Geese are friendly, inquisitive birds. ABOVE: Geese enjoying an afternoon snack of corn.

breeding

Timing

Geese need to be established in the autumn for breeding the following spring, as they need time to bond.

Breeding groups

It can be that a gander (male goose) will have nothing to do with some of his girls! This is not good if you want them to breed – this happened to me once with a gander called Honker, who only had eyes for a Muscovy duck!

For the heavier breeds of geese, such as Toulouse, one gander to three geese is a good mix. Lighter breeds, such as Sebastopol, can breed in groups of one gander to five or six geese.

Once your group has bonded, they can free range with other geese if you have them. There should be no arguments, as ganders are usually respectful of other ganders and the birds will usually stick to their own breeding groups once they have bonded.

Natural incubation

Geese are normally great mothers, but problems can occur if more than one wishes to sit, hatch and share the nest, as eggs will become mixed up. You need to date the eggs and remove the other geese to allow one to do her job properly in peace; this could mean finding a temporary house for her.

The actual incubation period for goose eggs varies depending on the breed. Lighter breeds, for example Sebastopol and Pilgrim, can start pipping (beginning to hatch) on day 28, while eggs from the larger breeds, like Toulouse, can take up to 35 days. Hatching can take up to 3 days to complete, so patience is needed.

Artificial incubation

All eggs used should be clean, undamaged and fresh. You can clean them with a special egg sanitiser – it is a good idea to do this before placing them in an incubator, as if any germs get into that moist, warm environment they will multiply. Eggs can be stored for up to 7 days before incubating – just make sure to turn them once a day.

Incubators should be disinfected and run for 24 hours before you add the eggs to get the temperature and humidity correct. For geese, as with ducks, the temperature needed is approximately 37.5°C. However, for geese the humidity needed is much higher than with duck eggs, around 55 per cent, so sprinkle or spray the eggs with warm water daily. These are guidelines only – read the instructions for your incubator as they vary. Make sure your incubator is set in a room away from direct sunlight and with a constant temperature, as this can affect the performance of your incubator.

If you have a self-turning incubator, you do not need to turn your eggs, but if you don't you will have to turn them by hand 3–5 times a day. Mark the eggs with a cross so you know when they are being turned; try to make sure that every night they sit on a different side.

Candle eggs (see page 71) at about 10 days and dispose of any that are not fertilised – these will be clear eggs. While candling, check that the humidity levels are correct, by checking the air cell.

During hatching, reduce the temperature to 36.5°C and aim to keep the humidity at around 80 per cent. The hatching process for geese is the same as for ducks (see page 112).

LEFT: Geese and ducks get along well, and are always interested in what's going on around them.

rearing

Rear and feed your goslings as you would ducks (see page 110), but after a week place turf in their box to entertain them. Goslings can suffer from hypothermia when they have their baby down, so protection from rain and wind is needed at all times.

health

Like ducks, geese are extremely hardy as long as they have good food, rotated pasture and fresh, clean water. However, there are a few specific problems to look out for:

Angel wing – This is when the wing sticks out at an angle. There is nothing that can be done to cure an adult bird. Although the afflicted goose can live quite happily with the condition, you should not breed from it as currently it is not clear whether angel wing is hereditary – this may affect whether you wish to keep the bird. In goslings, angel wing can be caused by too much protein in the diet, so cut down on this if you see any early signs. Geese get their protein from foraging worms and bugs, so you may have to control their foraging in order to cut down their protein. You can strap the wing into place – veterinary bandages are ideal for this. After around a week of using them, you should see if there is any improvement with the bird. If no improvement is seen, you need to decide if you wish to keep the bird.

Gizzard worm – If you are routinely rotating pasture, this shouldn't be a problem. However, if you are not, you may start to notice that birds are sitting down a lot, remaining still and have slightly glazed eyes. It is difficult to explain how the birds look when they have gizzard worm, but once you have experienced it once, it is easily spotted thereafter. For this, I find Flubenvet poultry wormer works well and can be added to the feed.

Goose = female
Gander = male
Goslings = baby geese
Gaggle = group of geese

CLOCKWISE FROM BOTTOM LEFT: Clear, bright eyes are a sign of good health; a clean, healthy beak; restraining a goose firmly and gently.

preparing for the table

Geese can be slaughtered using the same method as for turkeys (see page 89).

For instructions on plucking and drawing the bird, see pages 130–131.

Eggs for eating

Goose eggs are delicious. They are about three times the size of chicken eggs, so will obviously take longer to cook. They can be sold at your gate just as with chicken eggs (see page 79).

plucking and drawing

The guidelines below apply to all the birds covered in this book, with the exception of quails, which are covered within their own section (see page 101).

Plucking

Once you have done it a few times, plucking becomes very easy. I actually find it rather therapeutic; my mind clears as I methodically pull out the feathers. It is also extremely satisfying when you have finished.

I pluck by sitting down and laying the bird on its back on my lap. Start at the breast and pinch a few feathers at time (probably about 5 or 6, but don't count them!). Pull them gently down, away from the body, working against the natural growth. You need to be gentle but firm to avoid tearing the skin. On tougher areas like the back, legs and wings you will need to be more forceful; this is the time to imagine something that really annoys you! Feathers will fly everywhere when you're plucking. Remove the feathers on the body, both back and front, then the legs. Once this is done, you can make a start on the tricky part – the wings. Some of the feathers, especially on larger birds, will be really hard to remove by hand. I find a small pair of pliers can be helpful to get a better grip. I tend to snip the tip of

the wing off with shears, as there is not enough meat on them to warrant the effort of plucking them.

The end result will be a wonderful, clean, smooth bird with a ruff of feathers around its head. Don't worry if there are a few rips in the skin the first time you pluck; as you become more experienced, your hands will become accustomed to the correct pressure needed. Some people prefer to 'rough pluck' a bird (quickly removing the vast majority of feathers and not worrying about missing some), and then go back over it and 'smooth pluck' the bird, to catch any feathers they have missed. I prefer to pluck properly and thoroughly the first time.

All birds need to be hung after they have been plucked. You can either let them rest in your fridge or hang them by their feet in a cool place. Do this for at least 24 hours and for no more than 10 days before drawing them (removing the innards, see below). Hanging is done to give the muscles time to relax, making the meat more tender.

Drawing a bird

Drawing birds is not my favourite job, although my youngest son still laughs at the noises that are made during the process! Take your time on this part and get it right, as mistakes will be messy and smelly. With the bird's head facing you and its back

THE SMALLHOLDER'S HANDBOOK

facing upwards, take a sharp knife and make a small cut in the skin – just enough to expose the meat underneath. Once the cut has been made, stop, put the knife down and use your fingers to peel back the skin as if you were pulling the curtains back. Now turn the bird so it is on its back, breast facing you. If you look down at the hole that has been made, you should be able to see a small sack; this is the crop. If the bird has been eating, it will be full of undigested food. You need to remove this carefully by gently easing the sack away from the sides of the bird's neck until you feel it is loose, but still attached to the other end. You are going to draw the rest of the inside out through the vent (bottom) of the bird, so this needs to be free to move. You now need to turn the bird around so that its legs are facing you and you're looking at its bottom (!) with its breast still facing up.

Pinch a small amount of the loose flesh between the breast bone and vent with your knife. Make a couple of cuts in the shape of a 'V' by the baggy skin to enlarge the vent; be careful, as you don't want to cut any of the tubes connected to the vent. Using the 'V' you have made, gently place your fingers inside the bird. Use your finger to feel for the membrane that might be there; this should be broken with ease. You should be able to slip your fingers into the bird, following the line of the breast bone, and take hold of the gizzard – this is firm and round and will be the first organ you can feel. Gently pull it out as far as the tubes will allow (you can breathe whilst doing this), then go back in and gently pull the liver, followed by the heart – they should also be pulled down as far as the tubes allow. You can now start very gently and methodically scraping the rest of the tubes out with your fingertips. The very dark tube is the bowel track. You really don't want this to break, so work slowly and gently. You are aiming to remove the innards out of the back end, although they will still be attached to the vent. Now turn the bird over and really carefully cut the rest of the vent away so that everything gently falls out. Wash the carcass out under a tap and admire your wonderful chicken.

This process is the same for all poultry, geese, ducks, turkeys and guinea fowl.

Don't be daunted by all the information! It's like riding a bike; once you've mastered it, there will be no stopping you. You'll soon get much faster and be able to do it without thinking.

5
LIVESTOCK

For most of us, keeping livestock is what smallholdings are all about! I cannot stress enough the work involved in keeping animals correctly following the Five Freedoms (see page 48). As well as being a lot of work, it's also a huge responsibility. You need to consider how you will cope when the winter weather hits, when you or your animals fall ill, or if you simply want to go on holiday; you can't just up and go – your animals still need to be cared for. Sadly, I have heard rumours of people disappearing on holiday and leaving their animals to fend for themselves. This is irresponsible and cruel. If you are going to keep animals, you need to keep them every day, all year round – including Christmas Day! It can be physically challenging – are you up to carrying 20kg of feed across a field so muddy that the wheelbarrow sinks into the ground? Could you restrain an injured sheep? Can you cope with the early mornings and late nights?

You owe it to your animals to give them the very best care, so make sure you educate yourself in order to be able to provide it. With so much information and guidance available, from courses at agricultural colleges to advice from more experienced members of your local smallholders' club, there is no excuse for ignorance.

The physical, mental and emotional effort involved is a huge commitment, but ultimately one that gives you so much satisfaction and a real sense of fulfilment.

pigs

Pigs are very intelligent – it is said that they are the most intelligent of all farm animals. They are much easier to keep than sheep or goats. In fact, I would go so far as to say that, of all animals, they are the easiest to keep. There is a misconception that they are dirty. In fact, they like to be clean and tend to go to the toilet in one place in their pen, which makes cleaning up after them easy.

All they need is a house that is draught-free, clean and dry; adequate feed and water; an exercise area with some shade; and preferably a nice wallow pit for them to enjoy. Not only have I benefited from fabulous meat from my pigs, I have also had hours of fun with them, apart from the odd occasion when I have been left pulling my hair out because they have escaped!

Of all the animals I have raised for meat I do find, even now, that slaughter day is very hard. Pigs are sensitive animals and their eyes really do move you. Having said that, I gain huge satisfaction from giving them a wonderful life, which in turn gives me guilt-free, delicious meat.

RIGHT: Large Black piglets – these are fantastic pigs for a smallholder.

There are many pig breeds (see opposite), so you do need to do your research. Consider raising some weaners (young pigs that you rear for slaughter) before jumping into breeding. Gaining experience slowly and taking your time means you will have a relatively stress-free experience. However good your knowledge and husbandry skills may be, animals always seem to be able to throw something new at you.

A female pig will reach sexual maturity at around 6 months. Advice on when to breed them varies; in my experience, 10 months is about right, as by then they are large enough to provide you with a good-sized litter.

The lifespan of a pig is dependent on why you are keeping them. A breeding sow would tend to have around 4–6 litters before being sent off for meat, but I have known pigs of 6–8 years producing great litters. It is very dependent on the pig's health and breed. An average-sized litter is around 8 piglets, but again it really does depend on the pig's breed, age and state of health.

Pigs reared for meat are usually ready for slaughter at about 6–10 months, depending on what you require from them. Pork pigs for joints and meat are normally slaughtered at 4–6 months, depending on the breed. If a pig is being reared for bacon, it is kept slightly longer, going to slaughter at around 6–10 months, depending on the breed. There have been reports of pigs living until they are 25 years old, but I have never experienced this; I would say for a pet pig the lifespan would be around 10–13 years.

Don't worry if you're a few months late slaughtering your pigs. It's no big deal, it just means you've fed and cared for them longer than you needed to. This would be an issue for commercial farmers, as it would affect their profits, but for smallholders, where everything is a learning curve, it is simply a lesson to gain experience from.

LEFT: **Playtime for friendly Large Black piglets.**

THE SMALLHOLDER'S HANDBOOK

choosing a breed

Whatever the breed, a healthy pig should have the following attributes:

• a shiny coat with no redness
• clean ears (erect or lopped, depending on the breed)
• feet that are level, with no signs of lameness
• a nose that is moist and cold but not runny
• clean, bright eyes
• a straight back

I do believe in using your common sense to tell you whether an animal is in good condition or not. Do not, when picking your animal, allow yourself to feel sorry for one. My sister always does this and it usually ends in tears and a large vet bill. Buy from a reputable breeder who is happy to offer ongoing help and advice and make sure you are happy with the conditions they are kept in. When buying piglets, don't be alarmed when they scream – and boy, do they scream – when their feet are not on the floor. It doesn't mean they will be unfriendly or nasty – they just do not like being caught, and piglets are very noisy when not happy.

Think about why you want pigs. It might be that you wish to keep a few as pets and let them clear some woodland or overgrown land. You may want to specifically raise a purebred pig, or just have a cost-effective, low-maintenance supply of meat. Whatever your intention, there are a number of breeds to choose from.

Gloucester Old Spot – A large, hardy pig that produces top-quality meat for all purposes. They have large, droopy ears that flap when they run to you, and they are easy to manage as long as you are firm with them. They will thrive outside, as long as they have a warm and comfortable shelter. They used to be called 'cottagers' or 'orchard' pigs, as they were once kept in cider orchards and on dairy farms.

Tamworth – This ginger pig is one of the most easily recognisable breeds, with a very long snout, long legs which are great for turning over ground (pigs are great natural ploughs!), and pricked-up ears, giving it an eager, alert stance. The sows are great mothers and extremely hardy. Tamworths produce a lovely, white-fleshed carcass. As they are such good rooters (pigs dig deeply with their snouts, known as rooting), your fences need to be very sturdy.

Middle White – I love these pigs! They have a short snout, a dish-shaped face and huge upright ears, giving them a wonderfully magical appearance. They are quick to mature but not great to rear for bacon as they tend to put on too much fat. They are very docile pigs, quite hardy, and don't tend to root as much as other pigs due to their stubby nose. They have a special place in my heart but some people do not feel the same way, so it is worth doing some research.

Saddleback – A good grazer and a very hardy, genuine all-round pig that is equally useful for pork or bacon. Saddlebacks are easy to keep and extremely likeable with a calm nature. They sow (give birth) regularly, produce large litters and make wonderful mums.

Large White – A hardy breed that produces large litters. They are, as a rule, great mums and produce excellent milk for their litters. The breed was developed in England in the 1700s and has become very well established commercially.

Landrace – This is a large, long pig with lovely droopy ears. They are great mums, very hardy, and produce good-sized litters. They make lovely pork or bacon.

Berkshire – Classified as at risk, these are early-maturing pigs that enjoy grazing on pasture. The meat is slightly darker than commercial pork and has so much more flavour. They are friendly, curious pigs – ideal for a smallholder.

Kunekune – Often kept as pets and on farm parks where people love to see them. They shouldn't be overlooked – they are compact, friendly, amiable pigs that love human contact. Mine happily sunbathe with me (or am I sunbathing with them?). They are best slaughtered early, as they have a tendency to carry a lot of fat as they get older. They are hardy and very trainable, and make great, caring mums. The only real problem is that they are so adorable and friendly, it makes the trip to the freezer very, very hard. Great for a smallholding with limited space.

Large Black – Very gentle pigs with beautiful lop ears. They are very hardy, so are happy outdoors, and efficiently convert low-quality feed into high-quality pork. They are good mothers and produce large litters; they are rather protective of their piglets, so need mindful handling when with their young. As their skin is black, they are less prone to sunburn (pages 148–149).

Oxford Sandy and Black – One of the oldest British pig breeds. They are ginger with black splodges and used to be known as 'Plum Pudding Pigs' because of their markings. They are good-sized pigs, with lop ears and a long snout, and are ideal for the smallholder, as they can cope with most outdoor conditions. They are docile, make great mothers and produce tasty pork and high-quality bacon.

Mangalitsa – Once seen, never forgotten; they have a curly coat, rather like a sheep. They are one of the oldest European breeds, originating from Hungary. Their flavour is amazing, but they are slow to mature so won't be ready for slaughter until much later than other breeds – at about 15 months. They are hardy, great at foraging and will become extremely tame. They come in three colours: blond, black and ginger. For tasty meat, they are difficult to beat.

RIGHT: Clockwise, from bottom left: a large sow being herded with a pig board; an Oxford Sandy and Black sow with her piglets, which are a cross with a Large Black; an Oxford Sandy and Black piglet.
BELOW: My favourite pig, the Middle White.

THE SMALLHOLDER'S HANDBOOK

BELOW: My Oxford Sandy and Black piglets sheltering from the rain.

housing

Your pigs' house needs to be well ventilated, yet draught-free. Pigs use their houses to protect them from the elements – that includes the sun. White pigs in particular suffer from sunburn if sufficient shade is not available (see pages 148–149).

Traditional dome-shaped arks (see picture on page 139) made from plastic or wood and galvanised metal work very well and are easy to obtain; they are also easy to move. You can also use stables, robust sheds or barns, as long as the pigs still have access to a suitable outside area (somewhere with space for them to run, wallow and scratch).

Houses should be deeply bedded with straw. As pigs don't usually use their sleeping area as a toilet, you will just need to top up with fresh bedding, although any soiled bedding should be removed. Do a big clean-out just before winter and again in spring.

Fencing for pigs needs to be robust and secure, and you do need to use electric fencing. With their strong snouts, large, muscular bodies and sturdy legs, pigs are the tanks of the animal world. As they can weigh anything up to 100kg – sometimes more – that is one strong tank! However, if they walk into the object and think 'ouch', as with electric fencing, they will walk the other way.

There is no point doing a rush job on your fencing, especially with pigs. Trying to carry out fence repairs while your pigs are mid-escape is not easy.

I have found that the best method is to use permanent stock fencing (stock fencing is a roll of wire designed to be attached to poles) around the paddock, with two strands of electric fencing to section off areas of the paddock so the land can be rotated regularly. I keep my pigs in one half of the paddock over winter, and the other throughout the summer, then re-seed in the spring. Allowing the ground to rest in this way breaks any parasitic life cycle (see page 39).

If you want to keep only a couple of pigs to rear for meat once a year, you can keep them in a relatively small area of land – about a third of an acre (1,300 sq m), but it does depend on the type of ground and the size of the pigs. Piglets will need less land, but as they grow the space they require will increase. If you are keeping your pigs for meat, the ground will have 6 months to recover after they are slaughtered and before you buy the next year's pigs, and your burden of work will be significantly reduced. If you are keeping larger numbers of pigs and breeding them, you will need considerably more land in order to rotate it properly. As always, healthy land means healthy livestock.

LEFT: Electrified wire keeps pigs in their pens.

feeding

There are two methods for feeding pigs: either throw the food on the floor and let them do what comes naturally, or put their feed in troughs or rubber buckets.

In the summer, when it is dry, I tend to scatter their feed on the ground, but in the winter months, when the ground becomes muddy, I use rubber buckets that seem to be pig-proof – they also double as toys afterwards. Troughs can be used, but I find that, unless they are staked down, they will be knocked over. The drawback of staking down is that it makes the troughs difficult to clean, and they do need to be cleaned regularly. So I would recommend using rubber buckets instead. They are easier to remove and clean, and also allow you to feed the pigs one at a time, helping you to keep an eye on how much they eat. It's important to watch your animals eat, as one of the first signs of illness can be lack of appetite.

playful pigs

Pigs greatly appreciate toys. Horse balls are highly durable plastic balls that last longer than regular footballs, and pigs love them – they love to play in general. Peaches, my Kunekune, always grabs the hosepipe when I am filling her water trough and runs off very proudly with it – I think she just likes being chased! The time you put into your animals will reward you with lovely memories. The saying 'a laugh a day keeps the doctor away' couldn't be more true!

Water

Fresh water needs to be available all the time. Obviously, in hot weather pigs will drink more. You can purchase bowls that are designed to sit in old car tyres; I find this approach works very well and, as yet, none of my pigs have tipped them over. The tyres are also sturdy enough for the pigs to rub themselves on – pigs love a good scratch, but obviously are unable to scratch themselves, so they will rely on having something to scratch against. The drawback is that for two pigs you would need two drinkers to last the day and in hot weather they need topping up. This is not a problem if you are around a great deal, but it's something to consider if you have to leave the animals unattended during the day.

Troughs are very good and hold considerably more water depending on the size purchased – however, pigs do tend to knock them over while scratching. You can try to sink them down into the earth to stop this happening. If you do not have

THE SMALLHOLDER'S HANDBOOK

access to a mains water supply, consider buying a water tank and placing it near the enclosure. Fill it with a hose or collect rainwater, then attach it to an automatic trough. This is a trough that will replenish its own water levels whenever the animal drinks. It will save you a lot of time in the long run.

What to feed them

Pigs really do enjoy their food and it is very easy to overfeed them. They soon learn to come running over to you when they see you and will gaze longingly at you in the hope of food. I find that a good guideline is never to feed a pig more than it can eat in 20 minutes.

Overfeeding will only result in an expensive food bill and a carcass with too much fat on. The best feeding guideline is to look at the condition of your pig and the amount of fat covering her spine – this is called condition scoring. Run your hand along the pig's hips and backbone and mark the pig out of five based on what you can feel.

If the hips and backbone are visible, the pig is emaciated and the score is 1. If the hips and backbone are noticeable and easy to feel, the pig is thin and the score is 2. If you can feel the hips and backbone only by pressing firmly with your palm, the pig is normal and the score is 3. If you cannot feel the hips and backbone, the pig is fat and the score is 4. And if the hips and backbone are heavily covered, the pig is overfat and the score is 5.

Many factors affect feed requirements, but as a rule of thumb, pigs require half a kilo of pig pellets each day for each month of age, up to a maximum of 3kg a day. In the winter, pigs will use up more energy keeping warm and so require slightly more feed. If your pigs have lots of land on which to forage, you will probably need less feed as they'll be getting sustenance from their foraging too. Similarly, they will need slightly less if you are also feeding them any crops you have grown yourself. A sow

LEFT: Oxford Sandy and Black piglets enjoying rooting.
BELOW: My friend Luke's lovely Large Black sow and her piglets.

in pig (pregnant) or one feeding her piglets will require more feed. Pig pellets contain everything your pig needs and are favoured as the main feed for most pigs – choose organic or non-GM varieties. Manufacturers will give feeding guides on their bags. Remember to keep this feed in rodent-proof bins and observe the best-before dates; the protein, fibre and oil content will be fine but the levels of vitamins and minerals begin to decline once the use-by date has been exceeded.

Adding vegetables to your pigs' diet will produce a fine carcass of tasty meat, not like the bland meat you find in the supermarket. Since the outbreak of foot-and-mouth disease in 2001 there are now strict requirements on what you can feed your pigs. You cannot feed your pigs anything that has passed through a commercial or domestic kitchen, so don't be tempted to feed them any of your leftovers. If you have enough land, fodder crops, such as swedes, carrots and fodder beet can be grown.

Pigs love acorns and an acorn-fed pig is said to produce sweeter meat. Pannage is the practice of releasing domestic pigs into a forest so they can feed on fallen acorns, chestnuts, etc. It used to be a right granted to local people on common land. Pannage is no longer common practice in most areas, but it still happens in the New Forest in southern England, where the pigs eat the acorns that would otherwise be poisonous to the ponies and cattle.

Nettles are rich in iron and protein, so dry them (see page 40) and add to your pigs' feed. They are an excellent tonic for all livestock, as the roots and seeds are said to have de-worming properties.

breeding

If you intend to breed your own pigs by keeping a boar, you need to remember they can be extremely dangerous and if they smell a gilt (a young female pig that has never been pregnant) in season they can be very clever escape artists.
A huge, muscly lump of pig with only one thing on his mind can be quite a challenge!

If you wish to breed and haven't got the space for a boar, you could rent one for a set time, send your gilts to a boar, or use artificial insemination (AI). A vet can do this for you, or it is possible to do it yourself – but I do think that it is very important that you get someone with experience to help you the first time. You can purchase the semen online. The most important part is detecting when a sow is in heat. Signs of this include a swollen vulva that is often red in colour, with a stringy discharge. Once you think your pig is in heat, send for the semen. It usually comes in an insemination rod, which you then need to insert into the cervix. This is usually done twice (the second time 24 hours later). I personally prefer the more natural approach of using a boar – surely they can have a little fun if they're going to provide me with some wonderful piglets?

A young gilt will be sexually mature at about 6–8 months. Pregnancy lasts 3 months, 3 weeks and 3 days, give or take a few days either way. I move my pigs into a stable to farrow (give birth). Here they are safe from predators and confined if there are any problems. You need to provide the pig with ample clean bedding.

Farrowing normally goes well with no problems and piglets being produced quickly. They tend to arrive one after the other, with short gaps in between, and are then followed by the afterbirth. However, problems can occur, so if you are considering breeding pigs, find yourself a good vet and get some hands-on experience before you take the plunge. If you have any neighbours who keep pigs, it's worth

THE SMALLHOLDER'S HANDBOOK

asking them if you can observe or help out when their pigs are in farrow – this can give you an idea of what to expect when the time comes for your pigs, and advice from your fellow smallholders is always valuable.

Once the piglets are born, encourage them to lie in one corner away from their mum under a heat lamp; this will reduce the chances of them being squashed when she rolls over. Some people use a bar to separate the mum from the piglets; she can see them and they can go to her to suckle, but when they have finished, they usually trot off to the heated area. I prefer to take a chance on the odd accident as the pleasure both sow and piglets get from each other is magical. This is a personal preference – I just like the more natural ways – but you might find you feel more comfortable using a bar to separate them so you're certain no piglets will get hurt.

Piglets suckle very quickly. The first milk contains colostrum. This is full of high levels of antibodies from the mum, which will protect the piglets from infection and disease until their immunity grows. Most sows have 12–14 teats, so sometimes a large litter means that you have more piglets than teats. If this happens you will need to hand-rear the piglets as you would orphan lambs. Baby bottles work well for this. They should be sterilised (I boil mine for a few minutes). Buy a sow milk replacer and make up according to the packet instructions. The milk should be body temperature when it is given to the piglets. After a few days, the piglets should be able to drink from a small bowl. They will need to be fed every 3–4 hours for the first few days, then 3–4 times a day, evenly spaced, until weaning.

For the first few days after farrowing, keep the sow's feeding regime as it was – you do not want to over-stimulate her milk, as this could deprive her of calcium. After a few days, feed should be increased accordingly depending on the number of piglets.

rearing

The piglets will be happy with their mum's milk for the first couple of weeks, after which time you need to introduce a beginner's ration of pig weaner's pellets. I also move mine out on to pasture, depending on the weather. When you start introducing pellets for the piglets, you need to provide fresh drinking water that is easily accessible for them. Watch the piglets for signs of scouring (diarrhoea). At the same time, you should check your sow for any signs of infection, such as swollen teats.

You can sex piglets very easily by looking at their genitals. Obviously if you wish to breed them naturally, you need sows and an unrelated boar. However, if you are keeping your pigs for meat, they should be going to slaughter before they reach sexual maturity, so in my experience the sex doesn't matter.

Aim to wean your piglets by about 8 weeks old. The sow's milk supply will reduce as the piglets eat more pellets and take less milk. You can then either sell the piglets on as weaners, or rear them yourself to slaughter weight. They should be on their weaner's pellets up to 10–12 weeks of age, after which they can go on to grower's/finisher's pellets until slaughter.

Daily Care

You need to check on your pigs at least twice a day to make sure they are healthy and that haven't been up to any mischief, like damaging their pen. It's good practice to feed your pigs morning and evening. Pigs are very clean animals and rarely soil their bedding, but they do tend to eat it! Keep an eye on their bedding and top it up when needed.

Make a habit of always checking your fencing at feed time and, if using an electric fence, make sure it's working. Most fencer units have a light to let you know if there is a fault.

My pigs tend to use a specific area to go to the toilet, so I clean this area out once a week and pop the waste on the compost heap.

ABOVE: Lunchtime for the Large Black piglets.
RIGHT: An Oxford Sandy and Black sow with her piglets. Their father was a Large Black, so they are a cross breed.

It is easy to tame pigs and in turn make them more manageable, but one lesson I learned early on was never let a piglet jump up. It may be funny and quite sweet when they are tiny, but it is not when they are fully grown. I had this experience with one of my Gloucester Old Spots – she used to knock me flying! She was never aggressive – it was just something I had allowed when she was small, not thinking of the consequences as she got older. She also took to standing up at the fencing when she saw me coming! Not good for the post and rail fence at all.

health

As with all livestock, effective husbandry is the key to good health. Land rotation is not just better for the land itself, but for the animals living on it. Rotation, in combination with clean beds and good feed, can eliminate most problems. Remember veterinary advice should always be called for if you're at all unsure – it's better to be safe than sorry.

a good idea, although if you only raise weaners and your land is rested for 6 months, you won't need to worm. Although I rotate and rest my land, I still worm my pigs with Verm-X as it works well for me and the pigs love it. There are several products on the market, so see what's available and choose the product that best suits your pigs' needs.

Vaccinations

The vaccinations that are needed will depend on what you are keeping your pigs for. Are you raising weaners for the freezer, are you breeding sows, do you just want a couple for pets or are you wishing to show your pigs? All of these factors will determine what approach is needed. Talk to your vet, who will help to draw up a plan for you to follow. Make your choices and do your research carefully – you need all the relevant information in order to make an informed decision. Talking to someone you meet at the market who has never vaccinated his pigs and never had a problem doesn't mean that you shouldn't – it might be fine for him, but everybody's circumstances are different and a vet is the person to offer advice.

Worming

Pigs can suffer from various types of worm, including roundworm, threadworm, nodule worm, whipworm, sparganosis, lungworm and red stomach worm. The symptoms of worms include weight loss or not gaining weight, a lack of appetite, coughing, diarrhoea and loss of general condition. Worming is

External parasites

Pigs can be affected by lice and mange. Lice are easily seen, usually around the face or neck, and can be treated with powders, pour-on liquids or a multi-purpose anti-parasite lotion. If a pig has mange, it will scratch more than normal and lose condition, and its skin will become red with tiny pimples. The pigs may rub their skins to the point of bleeding and head shaking is also common. If left untreated, mange can cause crusty deposits in the ears. To treat mange, it is best to take advice from a vet.

Sunburn and heatstroke

As previously mentioned, white-skinned pigs can suffer from sunburn. If your pigs insist on sunbathing, sunblock may need to be applied. You can buy specialist animal sunblock online; I use Sunguard by Gold Label for my pigs, a brilliant product. Overheating can lead to heatstroke, which is a problem with pigs; they have a thick layer of fat to insulate them that can interfere with loss of body heat, and as they do not have normal sweat glands they are unable to regulate their body temperature.

Adult pigs can run at speeds of up to 11 miles per hour

THE SMALLHOLDER'S HANDBOOK

This means shade, a wallow (page 141) and plenty of drinking water is imperative. Signs of heatstroke include a dip in the pig's back, excessive salivating, panting and staggering. Prevention is easy and better than cure, so don't get caught out on this. If you do get caught out and one of your pigs suffers from heatstroke, do not try to cool it by throwing cold water over it. This will shock the pig and could cause it to have a heart attack. A fine spray of water is a good idea, as is fanning the affected pig with a piece of cardboard.

Mineral deficiencies

This should not be a problem if your pigs are allowed to free range in a traditional manner and have a degree of formulated feed. But sometimes newly born piglets can become iron–deficient. I have never experienced this, but the signs are hard to spot. They include diarrhoea (often of a greyish colour), slow growth and rapid breathing. If you farrow inside, as I do, for the first few weeks place turfs of soil in the piglets' pen daily to help prevent mineral deficiencies.

Mastitis

This can affect the sow after farrowing. The symptoms are swollen, hot, red teats that are painful to the touch. Call your vet, who will probably prescribe antibiotics.

RIGHT: Oxford Sandy and Black piglets enjoying the sunshine.

legal guidelines

In the UK, it is a legal requirement for your pigs to have their herd mark applied before they are moved from your holding. This is also the case in many other countries, but if you're outside the UK, do check your own country's legal guidelines to be sure of the regulations.

Pigs under 12 months can be moved without a permanent mark – they just need a temporary paint mark. Use a stock marker spray or stick. However, if the pigs are being moved for slaughter, they will need to be permanently tagged or tattooed (see below). Pigs over one year old and being moved to another smallholding, to market, for showing or breeding must be identified with a permanent herd mark.

A herd mark can be applied in several ways.

Slap mark – This is carried out with a pad with lots of pins in it that form the shape of the herd mark. The pad is at the end of a long handle. Use a spatula or knife to apply tattoo ink to the pad, but don't overdo it. Then apply the pad to your pigs' skin, leaving a permanent mark. Preferably the pigs should be marked on both shoulders. It sounds awful, but if you do it while your pigs are eating they really hardly notice; just be calm and decisive. I tend to do it a few days before they are due to go to the abattoir.

Ear tags –These are either metal or plastic and have your herd mark printed on them (not handwritten). The tags need to be able to withstand the slaughtering process, so check your chosen abattoir's guidelines. The ear tags should be applied just before the pigs go to slaughter, as they can occasionally be ripped out. The manufacturer of the ear tags will supply the applicator. Ear tags vary, so follow the manufacturer's instructions, but generally you place the tag in the applicator, position it on the ear, and then squeeze it closed in a swift, firm movement,

walkies...

If you have pet pigs, you may wish to take them on walks. Yes, I have walked my pigs! I stopped after a memorable occasion when Peaches found an abundance of irresistible acorns, filled her belly and then decided to have a nap. There was no moving her, so I had to sit and wait for two hours while she slept it off. Before you walk your pigs, walking licences must be obtained from your local Animal and Plant Health Agency (APHA) office.

leaving the tag firmly on the ear. It is something I have never liked doing and if I can get away with it, it is a job for my husband!

Tattoo – You can tattoo your pigs' ears with the herd mark. This is very easy to do and will permanently mark the ear without the risk of any injuries later on. This is done using a special set of ear tattoo pliers. You put the ink on the pliers and then apply them to the ear. The needles in the pliers pierce the skin, leaving a tattoo.

In the UK, you must notify the authorities in advance of any movement of pigs from your smallholding by obtaining a licence to move pigs, known as an eAML2. Contact the Electronic Pig Movement Service (see resources) for the appropriate forms, which must accompany your animal.

Once you move new pigs onto your smallholding, you cannot move any other pigs off it for 20 days. You must also wait 6 days before moving any cattle, sheep or goats. There are exceptions for showing, breeding and slaughter, so do your research – there is plenty of information on Defra's website. If you have any questions, ring your nearest Animal and Plant Health Agency (APHA) office.

THE SMALLHOLDER'S HANDBOOK

sheep

My experience of keeping sheep started when I was a young girl and a farmer gave me an orphan lamb to rear. I can still remember the pleasure I got from caring for him – and my mum's displeasure at finding him in my bedroom! She put a stop to that very quickly, and Barney, as he was named, was relocated to the shed. I soon learnt that sheep are very simple-minded animals. Barney grew into a gorgeous, large, wilful sheep, with no common sense whatsoever. He was, of course, destined for the freezer. I thought nothing of this, as it was quite a normal thing in my family and I'd grown up with it. However, my own children were older when they were first introduced to the concept of eating meat we had reared, and it took a little more getting used to. I've found that they are fine with it as long as we don't name the animals we eat.

As a family, raising sheep has enriched our lives with both laughter and tears (and occasionally tears of laughter!) and we have some amazing stories to share. There was the time when my husband was flattened by Jacob the ram (I did warn him!). Jacob had that look on his face that said 'Not today', but my husband was keen to trim his feet, and was determined that that was what he was going to do. Boys being boys, the inevitable happened, and the quickest won! Other moments of hilarity include my daughters being used as climbing frames by the lambs, or my youngest son's total consternation when watching his first lamb being born. There isn't a day that goes by that we don't have a giggle at one of the animal's antics.

RIGHT: A Badger Face Welsh Mountain ewe with her cross breed lambs.

Seeing sheep calmly grazing in a field is a lot of people's idea of heaven. They are indeed truly lovely to watch, but the fact that they can be seen grazing in all weathers on the moors or on hills leads people to believe that they look after themselves – they do not! In fact, they need a lot of care. Among other things, they need worming, hoof trimming, dagging and shearing. This said, they are great lawnmowers and produce fantastic meat and wool – so they are well worth the effort of keeping them.

Before embarking on keeping sheep, I recommend you do a hands–on course. There are plenty around and most agricultural colleges run them. Alternatively, you could volunteer to help a local sheep farmer/keeper in return for some of their knowledge. If, after doing this, you still feel sheep are for you, consider raising some orphans for the first year rather than trying to breed straightaway. This will enable you to become accustomed to their needs. Lambs bought in the spring will be ready for slaughter in late autumn, giving you the winter to plan your coming year. If you don't have much land, this is a very beneficial system, as your field can be rested over the winter with no worries about feeding or housing in bad weather. This approach will give you an insight into what is involved with producing your own meat – the whole process is not for everyone!

You should also consider all the financial implications. Your land will need to be adequately fenced, you will need to budget for the cost of your sheep and their transportation and be ready for any unexpected vet bills, as you never know what tomorrow will bring. You will need to purchase sheep hurdles, which are an absolute must when it comes to handling your charges for worming, foot trimming or shearing. Shelter will be needed during the winter and for lambing. Always budget carefully for the winter, particularly when it comes to lambing, feed and routine medication. If, after reading this, you feel maybe sheep are too much of a responsibility, you could always think of allowing someone to graze their sheep on your land; that way you have the pleasure of watching and listening to them without the responsibility and hard work.

FAR LEFT: Cross breed ewe and lambs. LEFT: Soay sheep. ABOVE: The beautiful Bluefaced Leicester sheep.

choosing a breed

We keep sheep for a number of reasons: to make a living from their wool, their hides, their meat and their milk. It is not easy to do it on a small scale. Hobby farmers tend to raise sheep for the home-grown meat, enjoying the benefits of producing their own food. Some people just keep sheep as pets to mow the lawn; they are very relaxing animals, and the most eco-friendly mower you will find.

There is no 'one size fits all' breed of sheep, nor is there a 'best' breed. It all depends on your needs and what you can offer in terms of pasture and time. Let the market and geographical proximity to sheep breeders help you make your choice. When all points are considered, a compromise will probably need to be made. Visit agricultural shows, do your research and visit breeders before making your final decision. When just starting out, it is often best to find somebody local to ask for advice. Pick a breed that is suited to your location and situation. Having a flock of large, heavy Texels might not be suitable for a small person who is not physically strong. I am not keen on horned varieties as I had a fright with a Jacob once and found the horns rather scary – much to the amusement of my husband, who was too busy laughing to help me out. Do not take on more sheep than you or your land can manage – five sheep to one acre (4,000 sq m) is about right.

The best way to start narrowing down your choice would be to ask yourself why you want sheep: as pets or living lawnmowers? For breeding, for wool, for meat, or perhaps to do your part in protecting a rare breed? As I mentioned above, each breed has different attributes. If you wish to keep sheep for breeding, for example, consider their ability to lamb and their mothering skills. The best age to buy for future breeding stock is about one year – sheep of this age are classed as a first time breeder or yearling ewe.

It is impossible to list all the sheep breeds but I have included a few to give you some ideas. It's worth bearing in mind that cross breeding in sheep is very common and, depending on the cross, can produce fantastic animals, so see what your local breeders have to offer.

Ouessant – Originally from the Ile de Ouessant in Brittany, France, they are the smallest sheep in the world, with the rams' shoulder height at just 48–50cm and the ewes' 45–46cm. The maximum adult weight is 20kg (roughly the same weight as a sack of feed), making handling easier. Two Ouessant sheep take up the space of one of most other breeds, which is great if space is an issue. They are great pets and lawnmowers, plus they produce a high-quality fleece and a small carcass of very tasty and not too fatty meat, provided they are fed correctly. They are very hardy, not inclined to jump fences, and their foot care is very simple.

Soay – Another small breed, with a shoulder height of about 50cm and weighing, on average, 25kg. According to the Rare Breeds Survival Trust, the Soay is an 'at risk' breed. They shed their fleece naturally in normal breeding conditions in the spring and the coloured fleece is very sought-after. Soay are found in two basic colours: the dark phase, which is a dark chocolate colour, but can vary from light brown to black; and the light phase, which is various shades of tan. Their carcasses produce lean meat with a delicious flavour. They are extremely agile and tend to scatter when scared, rather than flock together. This can make rounding them up a difficult, if amusing, experience, so is not for the faint-hearted. They are not impartial to weeds, which is a bonus.

Bluefaced Leicester – A fabulous breed! With its gorgeous Roman nose, this sheep has a rather comical look. Its wool is fine and dense and is highly prized for its likeness to mohair. Most of the cross-breed ewes (mules) in the UK are thought to have been sired by this breed. Bluefaced Leicesters are very docile and friendly, but, in my experience, they lack the hardiness needed when you are starting out caring for sheep for the first time. They are prolific mothers and frequently have triplets or quads; this means you really need a more experienced person to judge which of the lambs should stay with mum and which can take a bottle!

Southdown – A relatively small and easy breed to handle. They are very docile with a gorgeous 'Teddy Bear' face and fabulous fleeces. A friend of mine produces fantastic duvets from her sheep; they really are a luxury item. Southdown sheep are economical, producing fast-growing and meaty lambs.

Dorper – Originally from South Africa, there are two varieties of Dorper sheep: black-headed and all white. This is a very hardy breed and lambing is straightforward. The ewes are great mothers, which enables the lambs to grow fast and thrive. Their carcass has a unique flavour and texture, making it ideal for people interested in trying different foods. Dorpers naturally shed their wool in the spring, making fly strike maintenance easier. Dorper skin is the most sought-after sheepskin in the world as it produces a strong leather with an exceptionally fine grain.

British Texel – A large breed producing a large, good-quality carcass. They are extremely hardy and do very well in areas of poor pasture. The Texel originates from the island of Texel in the Netherlands, where it has been around since Roman times. It has primarily been developed as a meat breed.

Suffolk – One of our oldest native British breeds, this sheep has the ability to grow and finish quickly. This makes it quite popular with commercial producers; because the lambs mature so fast, producers are able to market them ahead of the annual seasonal glut.

Devon Closewool – Renowned for its flavoursome, succulent lamb and dense, strong wool. It is lovely and docile and easy to manage, making it ideal for the first-time flock master. An easy-care, low-input sheep that is very hardy.

Wensleydale – A large, long-haired sheep and visually very striking, it produces a fantastic, high-quality fleece prized by spinners. Wensleydales also produce a good-sized, lean carcass.

Balwen Welsh Mountain – An original Welsh rare breed that is visually striking and very versatile. This is a hardy, small breed – an average mature ewe weighs 40–50kg, a ram 45–60kg. They have excellent feet, require very little attention and do well with little supplementary feeding.

Black Welsh Mountain – A very hardy, undemanding breed producing premium-quality lean meat full of flavour. It has a fabulous black fleece, which has the advantage of not needing to be dyed for craft purposes. An average mature ewe weighs 45kg and a ram 60–65kg. As a hill breed, they are content with short rough grass. We once had a gorgeous Black Welsh Mountain ewe called Maisey who followed us everywhere. If there was a way out – usually due to one of my children leaving a gate ajar – she would make her way to the yard to find us. She was also a great mother.

BELOW LEFT: A British Texel. BELOW RIGHT: Balwen Welsh Mountain sheep grazing.

housing

Sheep can generally live outside very happily all year round, as long as they have access to food and water, and a field shelter to protect them from the wind and rain.

Sheep must be brought in before shearing if the weather is wet, as wool must be dry to be sheared (see pages 162–163). You will also need to bring ewes in before lambing (see pages 202–203).

In severe weather, sheep should be brought into a barn or well-ventilated large shed. You will need to provide hay for bedding and make sure water is available all the time.

When your sheep are outside, carry out regular checks throughout the day, especially when you have lambs in the paddock. To be honest, it is such a joy to watch lambs grow and play that it would be criminal not to take some time to observe their antics. Lambs are vulnerable to predators, so I set fox traps just in case and, if there are signs of predators around, I will go out and shoot at night.

If your smallholding is near public footpaths, pop signs up asking walkers to control their dogs. I have lost lambs and ewes to aggressive dogs who aren't being properly controlled; it still amazes me how stupid and irresponsible some people can be.

LEFT: **Cross bred sheep keen to get out of their barn.**

feeding

Before you start feeding your sheep, it is important to understand how they feed and how their digestive system works. As ruminants, sheep are characterised by their cud-chewing behaviour. They do not have any upper front teeth; instead, they have a hardened gum/pad against which the lower front teeth bite. Ruminants hastily bite off and swallow their food – mainly grass, herbs and twigs – then they sit down and chew the cud. The word ruminate is often used to describe 'chewing' something over mentally.

Many people wrongly think that sheep have four separate stomachs; in fact, they have one stomach that has four dimensions, the rumen, reticulum, omasum and abomasum. The solid food passes into the rumen, where it is stored; it then passes into the reticulum. Here micro-organisms begin to break the food down and it starts to form a ball-like mass (cud). When the animal is at rest, the cud passes back up the oesophagus to the mouth, where the animal chews it up thoroughly, mixing it with saliva that aids digestion. The food is then swallowed again and passes into the omasum; it then goes to the abomasum and it is here that gastric juices are added and the stomach's part of digestion is complete.

Sheep are grazing animals, so the most important part of their diet is grass – they will need to spend most of the year grazing. Grass is nutritionally at its peak during the spring and early summer months. Over the winter, when the grass quality declines, sheep need hay or silage, root crops such as kale, turnips, fodder beets and swedes, or pellet feed. Pellet feed will also need to be given at certain times of the year, for instance during the tupping (breeding) season, during pregnancy and when a ewe is suckling her young. Find a good feed merchant who will be happy to help you choose the best product for your flock.

You can get vitamin licks, which are blocks containing minerals and vitamins that the sheep will lick. I make sure vitamin licks are available all the time; sheep seem to know when they need a vitamin boost. I prefer to buy these in blocks that can be attached to the fence , keeping them off the ground, but you can also buy them in buckets that can be placed at ground level.

Hay racks should be used for hay and silage and are a godsend in the winter. Buy one on wheels so you can move it regularly; this will minimise the dry or muddy patches you get when the sheep gather in one place regularly. Most hay racks come with rain covers to help keep the feed dry – nobody likes soggy food. Troughs should be used when giving pellet feed and ideally should be low enough for access but high enough to keep out faeces. Clean the troughs out once a week with a good disinfectant, such as Virkon–S.

Fresh, clean water should be available all the time; galvanised troughs are great for this.

ABOVE AND RIGHT: Cross bred ewes and their lambs. Note the covered hay rack on wheels in the background.

THE SMALLHOLDER'S HANDBOOK

shearing

You will need to shear your sheep – not only to collect wool for sale, but also to relieve the sheep of their heavy wool in the summer, when overheating could be a problem. If sheep are not sheared they will become matted and dirty, making them very uncomfortable and vulnerable to fly strike (see pages 169–170). The best time to shear your sheep is early spring, before the lambing season starts. Shearing the ewes before lambing cleans them up ahead of birth and also helps the lambs to find the teats more easily. In addition, it makes the ewes eat more grass to produce heat; this will give them the extra nutrition that they need before giving birth. Sheared sheep also take up less space in the barn whilst lambing takes place! You should never shear a heavily pregnant ewe, due to the stress it causes them – about one month before the due date is ideal.

Some breeds need shearing twice a year and the second shear is usually done late summer/early autumn, aiming to give them around 6 weeks of wool growth before winter sets in.

You have two options with shearing: do it yourself or call an experienced shearer. If you want to do it yourself, you really should go on a shearing course first and gain some experience, as amateur shearers can cause injury and unnecessary stress to the sheep and themselves. It is not as easy as you might think and is a very physically demanding job. Nowadays, electric clippers are used almost exclusively. I have used hand shears in the past, but this is time–consuming and something of an art. My first shearing attempt left me aching in places I had never ached before – and I can't say the sheep looked that impressed with my efforts! However, with practice (and under the guidance of a professional shearer) I did improve. That said, these days I choose to use a shearer and believe he is worth every penny. My sheep are happy – and so is my back.

ABOVE: Shearing may look easy enough, but it is a real skill.
RIGHT: (From left) a Black Wensleydale, a Torwen and a Badger Face Welsh Mountain, all ready to lamb.

Sheep should be brought into an enclosed pen and must be dry before you begin; you cannot shear a wet sheep, as there is a chance that either you or the sheep could get an electric shock! Besides, you can't sell wet wool. Do not feed sheep before shearing. This helps reduce the amount of waste produced by the sheep – keeping the shearing floor clean helps to keep the wool cleaner. If you are using a professional shearer, have your sheep ready and waiting in a pen. They will come for you if you tempt them with a bucket of food but trust me, they will not come if they see the shearer. A small area either made of hurdles or a stable is ideal for a small flock. The shearer will not want to be chasing sheep around and it is also very stressful and unnecessary for the sheep; they will be happier confined. Shearers usually provide their own flooring on which to shear, but I prefer to use my own to minimise contamination; remember, the shearer probably does several flocks a day, so it is possible for disease to be spread. Provide an extension lead and have on hand any medication that might be needed for worms, lice and fly strike – this is an ideal time to administer it, as they are confined and restrained.

Crutching, or dagging, is when you shear a sheep around its rear end to remove the dirty wool. You can attend crutching courses which will get you used to handling sheep and give you a general idea as to whether you wish to go on a shearing course. Crutching is an important skill to learn, as it is helpful to do this to your ewes before lambing and preparing lambs for the abattoir in line with current regulations.

selling your fleece

Rules for selling your wool may vary depending on where in the world you live, so check your local government guidelines first. In the UK, if you have more than four adult sheep, you are required to register with the British Wool Marketing Board in order to market your fleeces. Some rare breeds are exempt from this, which allows you to sell direct to spinners. Fleeces are not worth an awful lot of money and their quality will determine the price you will get.

One year's growth of fleece produces approximately 3.5kg of wool

breeding

Rams and ewes should be kept apart until you wish to breed them. The time you choose to breed them will obviously depend on when you want your lambs to be born. The gestation period for a ewe is 5 months or 143–147 days. I like my lambs to be born at the end of March, when the weather is getting warmer and the grass is starting to grow – so just count back 145 days, and that is when your breeding season will begin.

A ewe will have her first heat cycle at around 6–7 months depending on breed, nutrition and weather – sometimes sooner. This is still quite young to start breeding, though: I feel a good age is 10–12 months, when the ewe is almost fully grown. If you breed your ewe too young, you run the risk of stunting her growth, producing small lambs and little milk. Stillbirths and miscarriages may occur, as can complications whilst giving birth – so it really is worth waiting those extra few months.

Choosing your breeders

Choosing a ram for breeding is a very important decision and time and care should be taken when making your selection, as he will have a 50 per cent determination factor in the quality of the offspring next season. His feet need to be in good condition, otherwise he will have difficulty servicing the ewes. Check his teeth to see how old he is (see page 169) and make sure his general health is good. Both testicles should be descended.

Rams can and do breed as early as 4 months of age. However, my preference is to use an experienced ram who has 'been there and done that', so one aged about 18 months would be ideal.

Ewes selected for breeding should be healthy and have good udders. Buy ewes with a good record of lambing and rapid weight gain. Again, check their feet to make sure they are in good condition. If you are a complete beginner, I would suggest you get some yearlings (aged 1–2 years) that have already successfully bred. This will make your life easier.

I've heard it said that a ram won't breed with his own mother, but the truth is he will breed with whatever is available, whether mother, sister, grandmother or aunt. So be warned, even as lambs they will need castrating or separating.

Flushing

Flushing is a method of feeding up the ewes before they meet the ram. This is done to increase the chances of multiple ovulations, which will result in more lambs. If possible, turn the ewes out onto pasture that was cut for hay earlier in the year; this will have been rested and allowed to grow on as 'foggage' or late grazing. Sugar beet nuts can be scattered on the grass. If necessary, worm the ewes before turning them out and take the opportunity to give them another check over, as handling them while they are pregnant is best avoided.

A lamb identifies her mother by her bleat

Tupping

Tupping describes the time when ewes are with and being 'covered' by the ram. It doesn't take long for a ram to service his girls – about 20 seconds! Crutch your ewes before tupping (see page 163) – this will make the ram's job a little easier. The ram should be fitted with a raddle block. This is a colouring agent attached to a harness, which is strapped to his chest. The raddle block will leave a mark on the ewe's rump so that you can see when she's been serviced. This allows you to work out a due date. Change the raddle colour after 17 days; if the ewe is then seen with both colours on her it is a sign that she did not fall pregnant the first time (once she is pregnant, she won't breed a second time as she won't be in heat). If this happens with several ewes it is a sign that the ram is active but is not very fertile. Additional feeding should take place during this time.

Care of the pregnant ewe is very important. She should be fed adequately to supply her with everything she needs to produce healthy lambs. Keep the feeding regime the same as when tupping took place, but avoid overfeeding.

About a week before your ewes are due to give birth, bring them into a barn or stable. This keeps them in one place, making it easier for you to observe them and look after them if needed. It also keeps any lambs safe from potential predators. Bedding should be deep straw and hay and water should be available all the time.

For lambing, see pages 202–203.

I don't let my ewes and lambs out until they are a few days old. After this time, if mother and baby are both fit and healthy, I will let them go out to pasture. If the weather is extremely bad I might keep them in longer.

RIGHT: Orphan lambs staying warm under a heat lamp.

rearing

Mother nature is amazing and, most of the time, we need to do nothing more than watch and enjoy lambing time. Occasionally, however, things do go wrong, and you can be left with orphan lambs. You will need a predator-proof pen with heat and lots of straw bedding. If the lamb did not have its first feed from its mum, you need to give it a feed containing colostrum, which can be purchased online. The lamb will then need to be fed by bottle with a milk substitute; again, these can be purchased online or from your feed merchant. Make the milk substitute up and feed according to the instructions – I usually feed my lambs four times a day.

I then introduce them to a bucket feeder, which is a bucket with teats that can be filled and left in the pen for the lambs to help themselves to. You need to let them know what it is by placing them on the teats the first time, but they catch on very quickly. Keeping bottles and buckets clean is very important.

From day 5, I leave them a small bucket of creep (lamb feed), which is a complete feed. They do not eat much at all, but it allows them to get used to it as they play with it in their mouths. Water should be available all the time in a shallow rubber bucket.

Weather depending, the lambs should be able to run around outside and enjoy the pasture. Do this for an hour a day to begin with and gradually lengthen the time until they can be out all the time; just make sure they have shelter from rain.

After about 3 weeks of grazing all day, stop milk, ensuring they still have access to water all the time. You should be aiming to wean your lambs off milk completely by about 12 weeks.

You can introduce your orphan lambs to the rest of the flock as soon as they are full of life and eating well (in very good weather, I have had them out in the field whilst still bottle feeding), but they will need to come in at night to protect them from predators.

health

All livestock should be checked daily, ideally morning
and evening. Take time to get to know your animals,
as determining what is normal behaviour goes a
long way in ascertaining their well-being. Visually
checking your charges is essential to pick up any
problems, and the quicker you spot them, the easier
it is to deal with them. Taking the time to observe
your animals' antics is also extremely enjoyable and,
with this close contact, you will soon gain their trust
and form a bond with them. If you go near them
only to handle or administer treatments, they will not
like you very much! This will make everything much
harder for you and for them.

Life expectancy

As a general rule, life expectancy increases the larger
the animal; so a cow will usually live longer than a
sheep. The life expectancy of a sheep is similar to that
of a large breed of dog – about 10–12 years. However,
this does vary – the oldest sheep recognised by the
Guinness Book of Records lived to be 23 years old!

Foot care

For sheep to be healthy they need to graze effectively.
If their feet are sore they won't be able to graze
properly and, if not treated, this will affect their
overall condition. It is imperative to check and
regularly trim their feet. Sheep grazed on rocky, dry
soil may not need as much attention as those grazed
on lush, moist land. The breed of sheep can also
determine the extent of care needed. Generally, foot
care should be carried out at least every 4 months,
but with a small, manageable flock, a check every
month is beneficial.

**TOP: Inspecting hooves regularly is important when
caring for your sheep. BOTTOM: You should trim your
sheeps' feet regularly.**

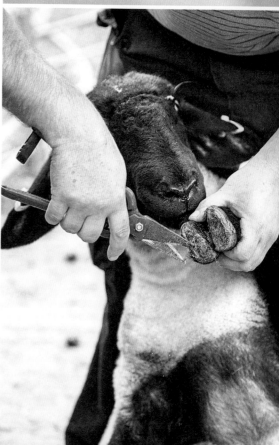

Lameness is probably one of the biggest problems faced by sheep keepers. Sheep's feet are split into two cleats (pads), which, unfortunately, provide a lovely warm area for bacteria to thrive and cause foot rot.

Scald is another extremely uncomfortable foot problem, and is caused by long grass irritating this area of the foot. When trimming your sheep's feet, take the opportunity to carry out any worming, shearing or vaccination; if you've got her penned or restrained you might as well make the most of it. Avoid trimming feet during late pregnancy or when it is extremely hot. Sheep coming in from a field that is heavy with dew or rain will have softer feet, making them easier to trim. Always trim a sheep's foot from the heel to the toe, using sharp, clean hoof trimmers or shears. I always clean mine between sheep. The first time you attempt it, I recommend you ask someone with experience to show you how it's done.

Teeth

You can gauge a sheep's age by its teeth. The upper jaw has a bony pad, the lower jaw has teeth. Lambs have 8 baby (or milk) temporary incisors. At approximately 1 year, the central pair of baby teeth is replaced by a permanent pair of incisors; these will be bigger than the other teeth. At 3 and 4 years, the third and fourth pairs of baby teeth are replaced. At that point, a sheep has a full mouth of permanent teeth. As it ages, the teeth will begin to wear and eventually break (much like in humans!). When a sheep has lost a few teeth, it will be known as broken-mouthed, and when all its teeth have gone, it is known as a 'gummer'. A sheep can survive with missing teeth but it is difficult to graze effectively, so additional feed will need to be given.

Vaccinations

There are several vaccinations available for sheep. The best advice I can give you is to talk to your vet about your flock's needs. Your vet will be aware of prevalent diseases in your area and will be able to design a specific vaccination programme, whether for ewes, young lambs, market lambs or rams. It is much better and cheaper in the long run to take this approach, rather than broadly vaccinate for everything just in case.

Worming

As long as your land is not overstocked and is rotated and rested regularly, you should be able to control worms. If this is not the case, regular worming may be required and a worming regime should be worked out with your vet. Signs your sheep may be affected are scouring (diarrhoea) and loss of condition.

I regularly use Verm-X as it is a natural herbal product approved for use on organic farms. Consider carry out a faecal egg count (FEC) before treatment to confirm whether your flock actually requires worming. This will reduce your worming costs, save time, reduce the stress to your flock and help slow the development of resistance to wormers without compromising the welfare of the flock. Your vet will be able to do a FEC test, or there are DIY kits.

Fly strike

Fly strike can occur at any time of the year, but is more prevalent in the warmer months. Shearing helps prevent fly strike as well as keeping your sheep cooler. As soon as the weather warms up, it is advisable to use an insecticide such as Crovect, Click or Vetrazin as a preventative. It is imperative to check your sheep regularly without fail, as sheep with foot rot wounds or dirty fleeces are prime targets. Fly strike occurs when blowflies lay eggs in the sheep's wool, hatching after about 8 hours – so it's a very fast-moving condition. Once hatched, the maggots burrow into the sheep's skin and feed on their flesh. It's a truly horrid condition, and one that most sheep keepers dread. I am totally paranoid in the warmer months and check my sheep regularly; this is made easy for me as my sheep come to the bucket and don't seem to mind my company.

If your sheep are affected, you need to clip the wool from the infected area, about 5 centimetres all around, close to the skin, then kill the maggots with registered chemicals. More than one application is required. Remember to collect up contaminated wool and maggots and bag securely. Very weak, sick sheep with severe fly strike may well require humane euthanasia, so speak to your vet if this is the case. Tea tree oil is great applied to any wound as a preventative to fly strike. It also has antibacterial properties and can help wounds heal, so it is well worth using.

Orf

Orf is a skin disease commonly found in sheep and goats. It causes sores around the mouth and nostrils, but can also affect other areas, such as the teats of nursing ewes. Orf occurs only if the skin has already been damaged, but even a small scratch can leave a sheep vulnerable to infection. The virus lingers indoors for years, so regularly cleaning and disinfecting buildings and troughs is an important preventative measure. Orf can also infect humans, so be careful when treating it or handling affected animals, and wear disposable gloves.

Orf will usually heal within 4–6 weeks without intervention, but if your sheep seems distressed or cannot feed, then of course seek veterinary advice.

Liver fluke

This is a parasitic flatworm that lives in the liver of some mammals. It can cause anaemia, weight loss, oedema and diarrhoea, reduced milk yields, reduced fertility and, in severe cases, death.

All grazing cattle and sheep are susceptible to liver fluke. Wet areas hold a higher risk. Prevention through pasture rotation is effective; it also helps if you can keep animals from grazing on very wet areas, such as river banks and marshy ground. Worming regimes should be discussed with your vet.

Condition scoring

This is an easy and necessary way of assessing how fat or thin a sheep is; because of their wool it is impossible to assess their condition by eye. Place your hand on the sheep's backbone and the short ribs that are in the loin area. Use your fingertips to feel the amount of muscle and fat covering the spine and then score the ewe on a scale of 1–5 (see opposite). I find it easier to do this with my eyes closed. The ideal score is between 2.5 and 3.5.

my first encounter with fly strike

I was looking after a friend's flock when I noticed that one sheep was standing alone in the shade. She was being very fidgety and stamping her front feet. This was unusual for her as she was normally the first to come over and say hello! Having walked up to her, I knew something was wrong; her wool seemed discoloured and her general demeanour was not right. What I found made my blood run cold – as I parted the fleece I could see the maggots eating her skin. Yes, I had read about this; yes, I had dealt with injuries and other horrible things, but this really tested me. I had to cut away the affected fleece and remove the maggots by hand. I was totally unprepared and had no chemicals to hand, so my husband purchased some Crovect on his way home. I applied it to the affected area and had the satisfaction of watching the remaining maggots drop dead and fall off the sheep.

THE SMALLHOLDER'S HANDBOOK

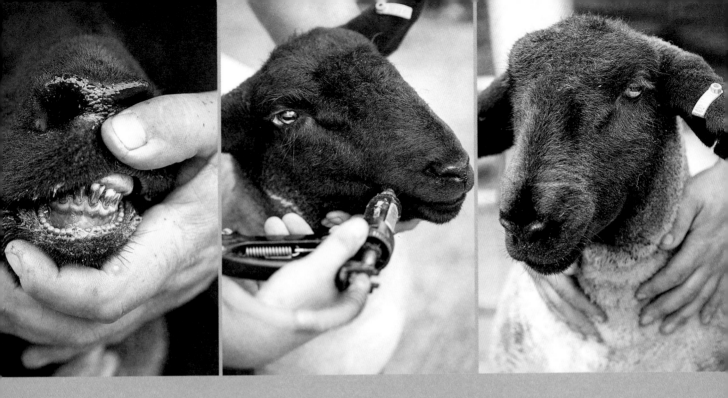

1 No fat and very little muscle. The sheep is emaciated. This is not acceptable, and she will be prone to disease and at risk of death.

2 Small amount of muscle but no fat. The sheep is too lean, which is an indication that nutrition needs to be reassessed.

3 Good level of muscle and fat, and bones feel smooth and rounded. Overall the sheep is in a very good condition.

4 Cannot feel individual vertebra, and instead the spine feels like a line. Lots of muscle and fat. The sheep is overweight, so you will need to cut back on its feed.

5 Cannot feel backbone or ribs. Sheep is obese and therefore too fat for slaughter. Again, you will need to cut back on its feed.

FROM FAR LEFT: You can gauge a sheep's age by looking at its teeth (see page 169); administering worming medicine with a drench gun; a fantastic Suffolk sheep.

legal guidelines

In the UK, sheep born after January 2010 are required by law to have a yellow electronic identification tag in one ear and a matching conventional tag or tattoo in the other. Otherwise, the legal guidelines for keeping sheep are basically the same as for other lifestock (see page 50).

goats

Quick-witted and quick-footed, goats produce fantastic meat and milk. You must have very good fencing in place, as they are great escape artists. One of my goats, Esme, became very adept at opening the gate to her pen – she watched me, learned how the gate worked, and conquered it. You should always be on your toes when looking after goats. Being one step ahead of them is better than being ten paces behind!

Some people have goats as companions for older horses or just as pets, but I feel that, on a smallholding, everything should be earning its keep. Goat meat is often overlooked, but it is low in cholesterol, high in iron and has less fat than chicken. Before you decide that you won't or can't eat a goat, I urge you to try it – and remember, it is a farm animal! The milk is said to be great for people with skin allergies and the cheese is delicious. Goats need less space than cows, which makes them ideal for smallholdings.

If you're raising goats for meat, the age at which they'll be ready for slaughter will vary depending on their breed, the weather, their feed and environment, but I would expect most to be ready at about 7–10 months. Goats can breed from about 7 months onwards, but I usually wait until they are about 12 months. They will give you milk as soon as they have given birth; I leave my kids to feed from the mum until they are about 8 weeks old, when they are weaned . I can then continue to milk the doe for almost a year if I'm lucky. Goats can live for 10–12 years – some have been known to live to 30!

RIGHT: Anglo-Nubian goats are sweet-natured and intelligent.

choosing a breed

Before you select the breed of goat you would like to keep, consider how much space and time you have available, and, most importantly, what you want to keep them for – milk, meat or fleece.

Anglo Nubian – This is a really sweet-natured goat and highly intelligent – once shown where to stand to be milked, it will not forget. It is a multi-purpose breed – it is great for milk production, producing the best milk for cheese, but also makes a fine carcass. The nannies or does (female goats) often produce twins, triplets and even quadruplets, and the kids grow quickly and put on flesh easily. The Anglo Nubian's distinctive appearance is another reason to love this breed: with its lovely Roman nose and big, floppy ears, it reminds me of Jar Jar Binks from *Star Wars*. It is one of the heaviest and tallest breeds of goat, with billies (males) weighing up to 140kg.

British Saanen – These dairy goats produce the most milk of all goats; they should milk about 5–10 litres a day. They have a calm, gentle manner, making them a great goat to start out with. Breeders often refer to them as living marshmallows! Being white, they are sensitive to excessive sunlight, so adequate shade is a must.

British Toggenburg – These are relatively small goats ranging from dark to pale brown. They have white markings that fade with age. They are friendly, alert and extremely active. They are popular with smallholders for good, persistent milk production.

LaMancha – These calm, hardy and manageable goats were first developed in the US. They are known for their small, shrivelled, almost non-existent ears. They are great for milk and produce a good-sized carcass.

Golden Guernsey – These lovely-natured goats are docile and intelligent, with colours ranging from pale orange to foxy red. Their feed intake tends to be lower than that of other breeds, but in spite of this they produce tasty milk with a high cream content. After the nanny goats have kidded and weaned, they do not always need milking every day; every other day will often be enough, as long as a routine is adhered to. A nanny will continue to milk well for up to 2 years without needing to be in kid (pregnant), which makes her very attractive for a smallholder.

Pygmy – These are miniature goats and make fantastic pets. They require smaller houses, less land and less food than other breeds. They are inquisitive, easy to train and handle and are very good at finding a place in your heart. They produce lovely meat, but obviously the carcass is rather small. I have never milked a pygmy goat, but I doubt they would produce enough milk to warrant the effort.

Angora – With their floppy ears and adorable curly coats, these goats are delightful to look at and they produce fantastic fleeces; Angoras produce an amazing 25 per cent of their own body weight in fibre annually. However, they will not produce enough extra milk for you, as it all goes into raising their kids and producing their wonderful fibre. They have charming personalities and are lovely to have around. However, if you breed and find you are left with too many offspring, the extras can be slaughtered for meat.

Boer – These are stocky goats specifically bred to produce great carcasses. They grow very fast and can be ready for slaughter from 3 months of age. The nannies make excellent mothers and are very fertile. Boers are docile, friendly and hardy, and cope well in damper climates, although they do not milk well. They are bred to have a shorter lactation period than dairy goats, plus they have smaller teats, which makes milking difficult.

CLOCKWISE, FROM BOTTOM LEFT: A British Toggenburg; an Anglo Nubian; a British Saanen; a Pygmy.

housing

Paddocks and fencing

The most important job to do before getting your goats is to sort out fencing. Goats are real escape artists; if there is a way to get out, rest assured they will find it! It is much better to invest the time and money in doing a good job of the fencing than to cut corners and find yourself constantly chasing after an escaped goat. I learnt this the hard way; I botched my first pen, watching the pennies, but every day I found myself having to patch up a different part of it. Hours of my time were spent retrieving the goats, nailing the posts and adding more wire. I definitely spent more money on that pen than I would have if I had just done the job properly in the first place – not to mention the time I could have spent looking after the goats rather than cursing them and hammering my

fingers! It was a good lesson learnt.

I recommend a 1.2-metre high stock fence for the perimeter of the paddock, with a strand of electric fencing at the top and one 15cm off the ground to stop the goats trying to go underneath the fence – they are quite good at crawling as well as jumping. Some people like to use barbed wire at the top and bottom of their fencing but, as I have already mentioned, I really dislike barbed wire as it can and does cause some horrid injuries.

If your goats have horns, use smaller-holed fencing, as normal stock fencing is a real killer for horned goats. They can squeeze their head through, but not get them out again because of the shape of their horns, leaving them vulnerable to dog attacks, heatstroke on sunny days and strangulation.

Posts to hold the wire in place should be solid and driven at least 60cm into the ground to hold them firmly in place, as goats love to scratch on things and may knock them over if they are not secure. Once your area is secured, you can use three strands of electric fencing to control grazing within the enclosure if you wish in order to rotate the land.

If you have any trees in your paddock that you do not want eaten, you will need to protect them by fencing them off. Remember that goats love browsing (eating leaves and twigs from trees and shrubs) rather than grazing (eating grass).

The paddock should be sheltered and shaded – like all animals, heatstroke is always a risk for goats in hot weather. Provide areas of interest for them, such as old logs to climb on, or old tyres, and change things around from time to time to keep them stimulated. They are intelligent animals and when they are bored they will look for things to get up to – and that usually involves something on the other side of the fence! As a general rule, a happy, clean, well-fed goat will stay put and be contented, in turn producing lots of milk, meat or kids.

LEFT: British Saanen goats enjoying the heat from a muck heap! Areas of interest like this are great for goats, as they enjoy climbing and exploring. BELOW: Anglo Nubians love interacting with humans.

TIP: If you are not using a mains electric supply for your electric fencing, you will find it extremely beneficial to use solar panels to recharge your batteries. It is easy to buy small solar panels that can be attached to your battery. They collect the sunlight, convert it into power and recharge your batteries so that they last longer.

Shelter

Shelter is very important for goats, as they really dislike rain and draughts. Ideally, the shelter needs to be within the fenced paddock and should be moveable. This way, when the ground outside the shelter becomes muddy, which goats do not like, you can move it to a less muddy patch.

The shelter should be big enough for your goats to lie down in and move around freely. As a rough guide, a shelter for two goats should measure 2 x 2m. Ideally there should be room for a hay rack. The structure also needs to be strong enough to withstand goats jumping up and nibbling the wood. Stable blocks make fantastic homes for goats, but you will need to walk them to their paddock each morning and back every evening. Goats prefer to be outside to graze every day, all year round, but on rainy days you may have to keep them inside and provide them with extra hay.

Drinking buckets can be placed on the floor or fixed in special brackets; the buckets drop into the brackets and are secure, eliminating spillages. Hay racks are ideal for goats and keep the hay dry and clean. Just refill the racks as needed. Never use hay nets with horned goats, as they will get tangled and stuck in them, which can cause injuries and sometimes death.

Bedding

Goats love a thick layer of dry straw in their sleeping area. Change it regularly – it will depend on the weather and the number of goats, but generally once a fortnight is OK – and toss the straw daily with a fork to check it is not wet; straw can appear clean on top, but actually be sodden underneath, and this can lead to a build-up of bacteria. Take out any wet patches and top up with fresh straw.

Cleaning

I do a big clean–out for my goats once a month, removing all bedding, washing the floor and drinking buckets with animal–safe disinfectant, and giving the whole shelter a good airing.

feeding

Like sheep, goats are ruminants (see page 159). They are browsers and really enjoy foraging for their own food. Half of their daily intake should be made up of foraged food.

I keep their hay racks topped up every day and also provide additional foods such as blackberries, brambles, elder and apple twigs, sloe, hawthorn, willow and hazel. I hang these on the outside of their shelter (or inside if it is raining), making the goats stretch to reach the branches – this keeps them active and interested. They also love nettles, so dry some in bunches and add to their winter feed. In the harsh winter months, or when goats are in kid or being milked, feed intake needs to be increased.

Goats should also have some pelleted food morning and evening. You can buy specific feed for your goats depending on what you are keeping them for, from starter rations, grower's /finisher's and multi-purpose pellets to show feed. These pellets ensure the goats are getting sufficient vitamins and minerals, but remember that they still need to forage and, during the winter months when foraging is harder, you may need to supplement their feed with hay. You can also get mineral licks for goats, which they enjoy, and will give you peace of mind that they are getting everything they need.

If your goats are browsing freely, please be aware that rhododendron, laurel, yew, bracken, foxglove, nightshade and ragwort are poisonous, as are some other plants. To be on the safe side, you should regard any cultivated garden plants as unsafe. Although most goats seem to know what they can safely eat, it isn't advisable to take the chance – there is always one that will prove you wrong and the consequences can be devastating.

TOP LEFT: Goats are lively and inquisitive, so their shelters need to be able to withstand them jumping up, like this one. LEFT: A Pygmy goat enjoying a mineral lick with a hay rack in the background. RIGHT: Pygmy goats devouring hay.

breeding

If you wish to breed your goats you will need a billy (or buck). Most smallholders who want to breed only occasionally will hire in a billy or use artificial insemination (AI). As with pigs, you can either get someone in to carry this out, or do it yourself (see page 144). If you take your females off site to visit a billy (buck), you will need to fill in the relevant paperwork (see page 50).

If a doe is in heat, she will wag her tail and make more noise than usual, from short bleats to long ones. She may mount other females and if she can see a billy she will parade around up and down and rub herself on the fence. If a billy is in rut, the boy can think of nothing else and will parade around his girls. Billies will also urinate in their own mouths – it needs to be seen to be believed! – and then spit the urine over their chests, beards and surrounding area. And yes, I have been hit! I stank for what seemed like weeks. Billies in rut also curl their top lip up, which looks hilarious, and make a very peculiar noise that my youngest son has managed to mimic brilliantly. I have to say I laughed so much it hurt.

The gestation period is 3 months, or 146–153 days. You need to separate the billy from the doe a while before labour is due as he will harrass her, and you certainly shouldn't leave him with her during labour or after the kids have been born. It is not fair on the doe to be pestered by him during this time and you will also risk him re-breeding too early. In fact, I generally keep does and billies separate other than at breeding time.

My first experience with a billy came when Luke, an experienced smallholder, lent me his billy goat George. I was very excited and prepared a lovely stable for him, all clean and smelling beautiful – I had even scattered dried lavender in his bed to help him settle in! I really cannot begin to tell you how bad he made both me and the stable smell. He was a lovely boy, well behaved and easy to handle, and certainly knew what he had to do, but boy, did he stink! He sprayed his urine everywhere and no amount of citronella could disguise it. I realised then that this was not something I would want around my smallholding permanently.

RIGHT: Don't be fooled – these aren't billy goats! Female goats like to playfight.

THE SMALLHOLDER'S HANDBOOK

billy goats and aggression

Despite their reputation, I have never experienced an aggressive billy and have only ever bred from billies that have a good temperament. A billy that has been well reared and socialised should be no problem if handled correctly. I have, on one occasion, been nudged and jumped at by a billy, but I did not consider his behaviour aggressive and actually realised his reaction to me was my fault for not being respectful. I had walked straight into his pen and started filling his water and feed without letting him know I was there. How would I react if someone just marched into my house without knocking? After that I learnt to approach him carefully and respectfully and make sure he knew I was coming in. Treating them thoughtfully and calmly goes a very long way towards having happy, productive and manageable animals.

rearing

The rearing process for goats is the same as that for sheep – see page 166.

Milking

Milking is so therapeutic – when you have a well-behaved goat, that is! You need to give her a small amount of food to eat whilst milking takes place. She needs to be tied up and standing in your milking area happily munching on her food before you begin.

First, wash her teats with warm water. As well as removing any dirt, this will help to relax her teats. Place your bucket under the udder, slightly in front of them. With clean, warm hands, wrap your thumb and forefinger confidently around the base of the teat and squeeze with your middle finger, followed by your ring finger and lastly your little finger in one smooth, flowing movement. Depending on the size of the teat, you may have to use fewer fingers. You must keep a tight grip at the top of the udder; this traps milk into the teat for you to push down. Relax your grip on the base of the teat after every squirt to enable the teat to refill. Do not pull on the teat too hard, as this will hurt the goat.

The first couple of squirts from each teat should be aimed away from the bucket into a cup so you can examine it for clots or blood spots. The first squirts will also contain dirt and bacteria, so should be discarded. After this you can aim at the bucket.

Continue milking until you notice the udders look deflated. Massaging the udders for about 30 seconds when you think they are empty can help to relax them, which may help to get some more milk out.

After milking, clean the teat using a special teat dip, spray or balm – there are a number of products available. Always wash your hands between milking different goats to prevent any bacteria being transferred from goat to goat.

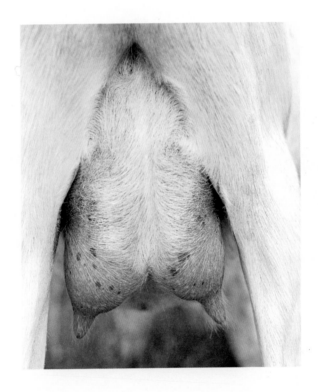

LEFT: **Pygmy goats feeding.** ABOVE: **Healthy udders.**

health

Health issues for goats are very similar to those for sheep (pages 168–171). They require regular worming and feet trimming. They can pick up ticks, lice and fleas and occasionally fly strike, a particularly horrible condition where blowflies lay their eggs in the goat's fleece. All these issues can be minimised through good husbandry skills. Goats enjoy being groomed, and this extra contact makes it easy for you to check for problems. If you groom your goats from an early age, they will be very amenable. A healthy goat will be bright and alert. There should be no discharge from the nose, and their coat should be clean and glossy.

legal guidelines

The legal guidelines for goats are generally the same as those for sheep (see page 171).

If you plan to sell products, such as cheese, made with your goat's milk, you have a lot of homework to do first. There are various laws and regulations that you will need to be aware of. They will change from country to country, but in the UK I recommend you start with the Food Standards Agency. They will be able to provide all the information you need, including current legislation and hygiene requirements. Your local environmental health department will also be able to advise you, as will fellow smallholders who have already been through the red tape.

ABOVE: Delicious goat's cheese made at the Norsworthy Dairy smallholding from their goat's milk. LEFT: Goats are very friendly and love company.

Like sheep, goats have rectangular pupils rather than round. This gives them very good night vision.

COWS

I love watching cows in the field, chewing the cud and taking it easy. They are calming and beautiful to watch, but keeping cows requires experience, knowledge, time and good pasture. It is hard – physically, financially and mentally. Getting first-hand experience with this animal is imperative before you take the plunge, as you need to know whether or not you can cope before you purchase any! Because of their size – even the smallest breed, the Dexter, is still a large animal – you need to be sure they are for you. My husband loves looking after cows, while I find them rather daunting, and have huge respect for people with the knack of making it all seem so easy. There is also a lot of paperwork and legislation involved (see page 201).

As with any animal, you need to know what you want to keep cows for before you get started – do you want to raise cows for beef or dairy, or try to do both?

In my experience, and through talking to others, I believe the most sensible option for a complete beginner with enough land is to start with a few 'stores' for meat. These are calves that have been weaned, usually aged 6–12 months; you then rear them on to finish them. The aim is to finish them as cheaply as possible. The ideal situation is to put them to good pasture during the summer and feed them on hay during the winter. They should be ready to slaughter for beef at about 18–24 months, depending on factors like breed, weather and pasture. To be successful, you

RIGHT: An Irish Moiled cow.

need to buy in healthy calves that are good for meat. Avoid the cheaper dairy breeds like the Jersey, as they do not put on enough weight for this to work. Take a knowledgeable friend with you, and ideally buy from a breeder, not at market. Buying from a good breeder means you can learn from them, but I generally avoid markets because when you buy from a market you run the risk of bringing common diseases home with you, as the livestock are kept in close proximity and so the risk is considerably higher. If you do choose to buy at auction, always isolate your new charges for 30 days before letting them mix with the rest of your animals.

Starting slowly will give you a good idea about cattle and whether they are suited to you and your land for the foreseeable future.

Rare breeds are a good choice for raising stores, as their sought-after meat will attract a better price when sold on, which can provide a nice profit. It's also very satisfying to do your bit to help a rare breed survive.

Cows drink on average the equivalent of
a bathtub full of water a day.

THE SMALLHOLDER'S HANDBOOK

RIGHT: A young Dexter being walked in. They are easy to handle – on a good day! ABOVE: A Dexter looking playful.

choosing a breed

As I have already said, begin by asking yourself what you want the animal for, whether for meat, milk (or both), or whether you just want to give a few cows a happy life. There are dual–purpose cows good for meat and milk, as well as specific milk breeds and specific meat breeds – or perhaps you want to keep purebred cows to show.

Always buy from a breeder who will have considerable knowledge and skill that he or she can share with you. Buy healthy cattle with good temperaments. They should be alert and have a healthy coat, clear bright eyes, clean nostrils with no discharge, and be free from hoof problems. Buying a cow that has been halter–trained and is easy to handle will help you gain confidence and experience without the stress! I've listed a few breeds that I think are suitable for the novice smallholder.

Dexter – This is the smallest breed of British cattle and is great for both meat and milk. Dexters are very hardy and are capable of living outdoors all year round, although they will need a field shelter that provides them with a draught–free bed. Keeping two cows to one acre (4,000 sq m) is perfectly doable with good husbandry skills. They are very good mothers, calve easily and produce lovely milk. The calves mature fairly quickly and make tasty meat. They are friendly and inquisitive, but some can be naughty and like to nibble! Make sure before you purchase that you go to the breeder and meet the cows; check out their personalities before buying.

Highland – One of the oldest breeds in the world. I have to say there is something quite magical about being in the presence of Highland cows. They are double-coated animals (their coat has a soft, woolly inner layer and a long, coarse outer layer) and can withstand fairly cold temperatures. They have long horns, so watch out when they come over to say hello to you, as they can forget they have them! They are easy cows to keep and handle and they do well on poor pasture, calve easily and are very intelligent. They provide wonderful, lean, marbled meat and can produce enough milk for a family.

Irish Moiled – Native to Ireland, this beautiful breed is easy to identify by its distinctive white and reddish brown colouring. They are medium-sized, with a mature cow weighing about 650kg, and have a docile nature. They produce delicious beef and milk well.

Jersey – If you want to keep cows for dairy, a Jersey makes a great addition to any smallholding. It is a very friendly, docile cow producing milk that is high in butterfat – great for making butter, cheese and cream. However, it is not good for meat. There is a farm local to me that produces the most delicious ice cream from its own herd of Jerseys – they look gorgeous grazing in the fields.

Cows will chew the cud for up to eight hours a day.

LEFT AND RIGHT: Highland cattle are easily identified by their long horns. TOP RIGHT: An Irish Moiled cow and her calf.

THE SMALLHOLDER'S HANDBOOK

housing and land

The general rule is you will need one acre (4,000 sq m) of good pasture per standard–sized cow. As previously mentioned, Dexters are much smaller than other cows and keeping two per acre is acceptable. Ideally, separate the land into paddocks so you can rotate and rest it. Do not be tempted to overstock your land when you first start out as you will over–graze and risk seriously poaching your ground. Poaching is the erosion of land down to bare ground by livestock, and will lead to poor grazing the following year.

Fencing needs to be sturdy, strong and about 1.2 metres tall. Protect it with a single line of electric fencing at the top to deter the cows from scratching or pushing against it; a fully grown cow can weigh around 750kg, depending on the breed – that's a serious weight to be leaning on a fence!

A solid field shelter is needed, ideally with a hay rack for winter feeding to give protection from the elements when needed.

LEFT: An Irish Moiled cow and her calf by their field shelter. ABOVE: Cows need to be mucked out daily when kept indoors. RIGHT: Irish Moiled cows grazing.

Bringing your cows into barns over the winter (most commercial farmers do this, depending on the weather) will help keep milk yields up and rest the ground when it is at risk of being ruined by poaching. Some breeds can be kept outside all year round, but land needs to be rested and looked after, so take advice from a local breeder. If your cows are to be housed over winter they need a solid, well-ventilated barn with a water supply, lighting and, ideally, an exercise yard. Do not think it will be easy – they will need to be mucked out daily and be provided with clean bedding, water and food. It will be hard work, but very rewarding. A separate good-sized barn will also be required for storage of feed and bedding.

At some point you will also need to have a restraining area for your cows so that they can have their hooves trimmed and medicines administered. These are not cheap. You can improvise with gates and stables, but be careful – you are dealing with a very large and powerful animal!

If you do not have a great deal of grazing space, remember that sheep can be grazed on the same pasture as cows. Cows prefer long grass and don't crop it very closely, whereas sheep like short grass – the perfect combination, as the sheep can graze after the cows have cropped the grass. Another advantage to shared grazing is that worm contamination can often be reduced – intestinal worms are species specific, so the sheep can eat the cows' worms with no ill effects, and the worms are destroyed as they are digested. Liver fluke is found in both sheep and cows, however, and needs to be treated (see page 198 for more on worms and liver fluke).

THE SMALLHOLDER'S HANDBOOK

feeding

Like sheep, cows are ruminants, so they require a lot of grazing, from spring through to autumn. Some cattle can be out all year round: it depends on your weather and land. During their outside months, all they need is good pasture, but once it stops growing in the autumn they will need to be fed hay. If you have enough land to grow and harvest your own hay, that's fantastic; if not, you will need to buy in hay and store it. Always order more than you need; there is nothing worse than running out in bad weather and having to battle through snow to obtain more. Fodder crops, such as leafy turnips, kale and swedes can be added and cattle cubes (complete cattle feed with all the required vitamins and minerals) can be purchased and used in addition to hay.

Feeding requirements vary depending on the breed, the climate, and whether the cow is in calf or lactating. A general rule is one bale of hay per cow per day. Having a mineral lick available all the time will give you peace of mind that your cows are getting adequate vitamins and minerals. A lot of health problems can be avoided this way. For example, early spring grass can lack adequate magnesium levels, which can lead to hypomagnesaemia, otherwise called 'grass staggers' or tetany. This is especially common in lactating cows, and its symptoms include an uneven, uncoordinated gait (hence the name 'grass staggers'). However, if a mineral lick is available to your cows, this should make up for any magnesium lacking in the grass.

Cows consume water in considerable quantities, so a good water supply is a must – especially in hot weather, when they drink even more. Automatic drinkers (troughs that automatically refill themselves) are helpful, but will need to be linked up to a water source. In freezing weather, you will need to defrost pipes and break ice to ensure your cows still have access to sufficient water.

milking a cow

The idea of a 'pet' cow to provide your family with milk often creates a romantic picture in one's head! And it's true, there is something so satisfying and fulfilling about drinking your own utterly delicious milk. But in reality, it is a very big commitment. You need the ability and confidence to handle a very large animal, not to mention dedication to the cause – you will have to milk her twice a day at 12-hour intervals without fail, or she will not be happy; swollen udders will cause her pain.

Cows produce a lot of milk, so you will need a clean area to process your milk – preferably one that is covered, as milking in the mud and pouring rain is not fun! You will also need to have a competent person to cover milking duties for you if you wish to go away.

Remember, for a cow to produce milk she will need to be calved every year, so unless you keep a bull, you will need to arrange artificial insemination (AI). When the calf is just born, the cow produces a small amount of milk, which increases as the calf's demands grow, tailing off at about 10 months when she will have a rest (dry period) until the next calf is born. For the absolute beginner, the best advice I can give is to buy a well-handled cow that has already been hand-milked, so she knows what she's doing even if you don't. Try and buy one with her calf so she has some company; she will produce enough milk for you and the calf. Cows are herd animals and need the company of their own species. Dexter and Jersey are very good for home milking and can be crossed with a meat breed to produce a calf that could end up in the freezer!

If you have never milked a cow before, ask the farmer you are buying from to show you how. It's not difficult and is actually rather relaxing. The method is the same as that for milking goats (see page 183).

If you have a smallholding, you will probably produce just enough milk to have milk, butter and cheese for home use. It's very unlikely you would produce enough to sell. However, if you are in a position to sell your produce you have a huge amount of homework to do. There are a large number of rules and regulations, and you will be monitored to ensure that you adhere to health and safety standards. In the UK, you can find out more by visiting www.food.gov.uk, where there is a huge amount of helpful information. You will need to attend food hygiene courses and speak to your local Environmental Health and Trading Standards offices… all in all, a huge amount of work! I would recommend you get to grips with your animals first and go from there. Don't try to do everything at once.

Cows do not bite grass; they actually curl their tongue around the grass and pull it up

THE SMALLHOLDER'S HANDBOOK

breeding

If you are completely new to cattle, I wouldn't recommend rushing into breeding. Get to know your cattle and gain some confidence. Keeping a bull is not really an option on a smallholding. Their considerable size means they can be extremely dangerous. If you have ever been to an agricultural show, you will have seen some amazing bulls – absolutely huge and surprisingly, incredibly relaxed. That is because they are looked after by experienced, knowledgeable herdsmen with years of practice and skill. In the wrong hands, and with inadequate fencing, a bull could do serious damage. Artificial insemination (AI) is a much better option (see page 144). You will know your heifer is in heat (known as bulling) as she will become restless and chatty and she may try to mount the other girls. The vulva will swell and have a clear discharge. My husband's favourite cow, Rollo, used to become rather amorous towards him around this time and, although she wasn't being horrid, needed careful handling.

When a heifer is about 16 months old and in heat, she can be mated for the first time. Before mating and during pregnancy, cows need to be in the best of health, so vitamins and good feed are vital. Pregnancy lasts around 9.5 months. About a month before her due date, her udders will drop and begin to fill out – a sign that calving is imminent. The first signs of labour are a shuddering of muscles on each side of the tail. The vagina and vulva dilate and a plug of mucus is released. Your cow will become restless and want to be on her own. If the weather is good, calving can quite happily take place in the field, and often

does. If you choose to bring your cow inside, the area should be thoroughly cleaned and disinfected and have a good layer of clean, dry straw. Normally calving is straightforward, but always have your vet's telephone number on hand. I let my vet know in advance when my animals are due – it makes me feel prepared! Once the calves are born, leave them in peace with their mother to bond and feed.

RIGHT: A gorgeous Irish Moiled cow.

rearing

Some people buy in calves that are not yet weaned, which means they require bottle-feeding. This will test you and, unless you have a knowledgeable friend nearby who is willing to help, I would avoid this until you have more skill. Humans make poor substitutes as far as the calf is concerned – nature intended them to be with their mother. However, if this is a route you wish to take, make sure the calf you buy is healthy and alert. They will need to be fed regularly with a good milk substitute. Hygiene needs to be a priority as calves can suffer from scour (diarrhoea, see page 198). They should be kept in a warm, draught-free barn with lots of clean, dry straw.

At about 5–6 weeks, you need to teach your calf to drink from a bucket. This can be done by placing your hand in the bucket with the milk and wiggling your fingers so the calf sucks at them. They may sneeze and cough a little at first until they get used to it. Slowly remove your hand; they will soon learn to drink. My husband loves this job and is a dab hand at it.

Hay, water and calf concentrate pellets should be available from about 10 days onwards in addition to milk. By about 6 weeks, the calf can be gradually weaned from the milk (cut the amount down gradually over a week) until only hay and calf weaner rations are available and, of course, fresh clean water. At this stage, grazing on good pasture can begin if the weather is mild, but only for a couple of hours a day to avoid scouring. After a couple of weeks you can gradually extend their pasture time.

If you get on well rearing cattle for meat, you will almost certainly progress to breeding a suckler herd – this is a herd of cows that do not require milking. The calves remain with their mothers, who will do a very good job of rearing them for you. They should grow quickly and healthily as having all their mother's milk to themselves will give them the best start possible. I love watching them together; cows are truly attentive mothers. For this reason you should be careful when handling them or going into the field as they can be extremely protective of their young.

LEFT AND BELOW: Observing the bond between a mother and her calf is a wonderful experience.

health

As with all livestock, health problems do occur but with good husbandry skills, hygiene and food you can eliminate most of them. When keeping cows you must register with a vet who can advise you on any local problems, arrange bovine tuberculosis (TB) testing and can also draw up a care plan for your livestock. This is very helpful for the complete novice.

Worming

The problem of internal parasites can be kept in check as long as land is rotated regularly and not overstocked. If you suspect worms, ask your vet to do a worm count on your land, which will determine whether you have a problem that needs treating. Using chemicals regularly may increase the resistance to certain drugs, although Verm-X is an excellent natural wormer. As I mentioned earlier, grazing sheep and cows together is advantageous when it comes to preventing worms, but does not deal with liver fluke (see below). The symptoms of a worm problem are a dull coat, persistent cough and scouring (see right).

Liver fluke

Like sheep, cattle can suffer from liver fluke. For more information, see page 170.

Lice

Lice can be a problem for cattle. They cause skin irritation; other symptoms include a dull coat and reduced appetite. They are often a problem in winter, when the cows have a nice thick coat – perfect for lice to live in. Lice in cows can be controlled with pour-on or spray-on treatments.

Mites

An infestation of mites is called mange. Cows will show signs of hair loss and thickening of the skin. Mites burrow and hide under the skin, making it difficult to control. Consult your vet, who will probably do a skin scrape to see what mites you are dealing with and prescribe the appropriate treatment.

Flies

Flies can be a real problem in the hotter months, so providing shade is essential. I use tarpaulin soaked in citronella, which is a fly repellent. Scouring (see below) will attract flies, so every effort should be made to avoid it. If scouring is a problem, wash the back legs and tail area to clean away faeces and keep the flies away.

Scouring

Scouring is diarrhoea in cattle. It can be caused by too much lush grass in the spring, so restricting their grazing for a while is a good idea. If scouring is accompanied by poor skin condition, it could be an indication of worms. Make sure plenty of water is available, ideally with hydration salts added to prevent dehydration. If scouring continues after a couple of days, contact your vet; it could be caused by a bacteria that will need antibiotics. It can be prevented with a vaccination.

Mastitis

This is a common problem in dairy herds, so making hygiene a priority while milking is very important. It is caused by bacteria getting into the cow's teat,

Cattle are red/green colour blind.

THE SMALLHOLDER'S HANDBOOK

ABOVE: Healthy Dexter (left) and Irish Moiled (right) cows.

causing an infection, and the symptoms include painful swollen udders. The bacteria can come from flies (especially when the weather is hot and humid), dirty bedding and poor hygiene during milking.

Cows with mastitis will also suffer from a fever. Fever can be easily detected by just observing your girls: they may shiver, show a loss of appetite and appear depressed – and yes, it is possible for a cow to look sad!

The treatment is usually an antibiotic flush, which your vet can show you how to administer. There are also homeopathic remedies that are worth a try. Tonics made of seaweed extract, cider vinegar and garlic in your animals' water helps build up their immunity, but always seek a vet's advice.

legal guidelines

The paperwork for cattle is far more complicated than with other livestock. It will vary from country to country, so if you are outside the UK, check your own government guidelines.

In the UK, you need your CPH number (see page 50) and you also need to register as a keeper with your Animal and Plant Health Agency (APHA) office. They will issue you with a herd mark, and you need this to buy ear tags. You then need to register with the British Cattle Movement Service (BCMS). Their Cattle Tracing System (CTS) is a database that records births, deaths and movements. You need to apply for a unique identification number and a 'passport' for your calf within 27 days of birth – this can be done online through the CTS website. You must keep this passport safe. If you sell the cattle, it will need to be handed to the new keeper.

Any movements of your cattle need to be reported within 3 days; keep your own records either on a computer or in a log book.

All cattle born after 1 January 1998 must have an official ear tag with the same unique number as in their passport in each ear; this is called double tagging. The main tag must be made of yellow plastic while the second tag can be plastic or metal. The manufacturers that supply these Defra–approved ear tags are usually very helpful and can advise you accordingly.

As of 1 January 2013, routine herd surveillance testing now takes place on farms in counties in the southwest, west country and east Sussex, where the most cases of bovine tuberculosis have been found. These will be tested annually while the rest of England is tested on a 4–yearly programme (unless you have a higher risk herd in this area and then they will be tested annually). This is carried out at Defra's expense. TB testing also needs to be done whenever you move your cattle between holdings and markets. When you register your cattle, you will receive a cattle keeper's handbook that will give you a lot of detailed, up–to–date information. Go to the Defra website to find out more or, better still, talk to your vet.

LEFT: A Dexter cow with an ear tag.

Cows can live for more than 20 years.

farrowing, lambing, kidding and calving

Breeding is truly amazing and emotional. The experience of bringing new life into this world is a hard thing to beat, but when things go wrong – which they can, even if you have done everything right – it is truly numbing. Before attempting to breed your own livestock, gain as much knowledge and experience as you can. You are responsible for your animals' well-being and breeding without any knowledge is a no-no – it is, after all, the animal that will suffer if things go wrong. You should be registered with a farm vet just in case things do not go to plan. You may also be able to get help and advice from experienced, local smallholders. Most animals give birth without any assistance or problems, but you do need to be prepared.

I can still remember the feeling of utter helplessness when my goat Dolly had a difficult time giving birth. I phoned the vet, who was unfortunately at another emergency call and wouldn't be able to get to me for 2 hours! Luckily, Luke, an extremely experienced farmer and friend, was on the end of the phone to calm me down. 'Just close your eyes and feel what is going on,' he advised. So I calmed myself down, inserted my hand into Dolly, and did just that. Dolly's kid was in the breach position, with the bum coming out first, but the legs were bent forward, so I gently manipulated the kid while it was still inside her and delivered him safely. The feeling of relief was huge and it was all down to Luke's calming advice. It is like everything in life – you learn as you go and gain experience and knowledge daily, but it is something you should not attempt without basic knowledge and support.

LEFT: An Irish Moiled calf. RIGHT: Pygmy goats.

There is quite a list of things you will need to keep on hand for birthing.

- lubricating jelly, in case you need to assist
- iodine to disinfect your hands
- dry pieces of clean towel to wipe things down
- navel dressing and spray or dip (see Glossary, page 220)
- heat lamp, to keep the newborns warm if anything happens to the mum
- milking supplements, bottles and teats, in case hand-rearing is required
- mobile phone in case you need to ring someone for assistance
- torch (a head torch is best, as this way your hands will be free)

The list of equipment is quite extensive, so if you are a first-timer my advice would be to call a vet if problems occur and learn and gather equipment as you go.

When birthing is close, the animal's udder or teats will begin to feel hard and the vulva will become loose and swollen. Pigs will make nests, which can be very impressive. Some people leave their animals to give birth in the field, but I prefer to bring mine into a stable a week before they are due so I can keep an eye on them – and also to prevent the predators taking the young. I once lost four piglets in the night to foxes!

When birth is imminent, you will see a clear liquid coming from the vulva and the appearance of a water bag (a very thin transparent skin filled with fluid). The baby then follows. The length of labour varies, so watch your animal's behaviour for signs of distress or tiredness.

When the baby is born, mum will normally lick it clean. Leave them to get on with bonding and enjoy the atmosphere. Don't be too downhearted if things go wrong – sometimes they do, even if you have done everything you can. Mother Nature tests us constantly to make us better people! I have had some

heart-breaking births that really took the wind out of my sails but I carried on, because when everything does go to plan, your wonderful, happy, well cared-for animals make everything worth it.

In the UK, you have to record the birth of any farm animal in the holding register. This can be done online or by post. You will also need to arrange ear tags for the newborn – the age at which this needs to be done varies from animal to animal, so check the Defra website to see which applies to you.

transport and slaughter

transporting livestock

Livestock are usually transported by trailer. You need one only when you are collecting newly purchased animals or moving them off your land (e.g. taking them to the abbatoir), so you may decide it is more cost effective to hire one when needed than to buy one.

There are a number of welfare regulations to abide by when transporting livestock. Rules vary according to the distance/duration of travel. As a smallholder, you are unlikely to be transporting your animals over long distances, so I have focused on shorter journeys. Even so, there are many things to consider beforehand.

- The animals should be fit and old enough to travel –you shouldn't transport very young animals (particularly newborns without fully healed navels), heavily pregnant females (unless instructed to do so by a vet), new mothers, or sick or injured animals (again, unless instructed). It is illegal to transport animals that aren't fit for travel.

- A competent person should always travel with them. For shorter journeys (in the UK, this is anything under 65km), the driver does not require a certificate of competence, but it is best for the animals' well-being that they travel with someone competent who will be able to care for them calmly and effectively throughout their journey.

- The trailer should have adequate loading and unloading facilities and be of a good size and design to avoid injury or distress to the animals.

Guidelines for the trailer's size vary depending on the animal, but you should always check these and make sure that your trailer complies – for example, current UK guidelines require a space of 0.95–1.3 sq m for each medium-sized cow you transport. There are also species-specific guidelines on ramp angles, height, etc., so be sure to familiarise yourself with these. The trailer should also be clean and easily disinfected.

- Water, feed and rest must be given as needed. Depending on the journey length, your animals must have access to the sustenance they require. Again, there are relevant guidelines for each species.

- Animals should be grouped according to their age, sex and species.

- The temperature and ventilation of the trailer must be suitable for the animals being transported. Transporting animals on a very hot day means providing extra water and shade, whilst cold weather may mean you need to supply extra bedding for warmth. You should not transport shorn sheep in very cold weather.

I strongly recommend that you read up on government guidelines before transporting your livestock to ensure that you have the relevant certificates, equipment and facilities in place. See Resources for more information.

keeping calm…

I find Rescue Remedy helps calm my animals before I move them. I also sprinkle lavender in the trailer – I don't know whether it makes a lot of difference but it makes me feel happier.

slaughter

Autumn is usually the time of year when my livestock are ready to be dispatched, and it is a very sad time. Animals bring life to a smallholding and the landscape becomes still and rather soulless without them. But it's important to remember that this is what smallholding is all about – and after the initial shock, a freezer full of meat cheers you up. Many people are horrified that I eat my own livestock, which I find very difficult to understand. My animals are loved, well cared-for and fed a natural diet; they can also run, roll and play, which is more than can be said for most animals destined to become supermarket meat. I enjoy eating meat, but do not want to be part of the intensive rearing of animals, as I believe we have no right to treat animals in such a way. Therefore, for me, eating my own livestock is kinder to animals than eating supermarket-bought meat.

I wish it were easier for more people to experience the pleasures of rearing your own food. It is hard work, takes time and money, and can be emotionally draining, but it gives you such a sense of belonging to the land and community – something that is sadly missing in modern society.

So although it can be sad to say goodbye to a much-loved pig or a favourite cow, there is a great sense of fulfilment from having given an animal a calm, contented life, whilst providing delicious food for your own family.

Home slaughter

Home slaughter is my preferred choice. I have an experienced, licensed slaughterman who comes and does the deed. The first time I had my sheep slaughtered in this way was traumatic for me, but not for the sheep – they knew nothing about it. They followed me one at a time into the yard for breakfast (a routine I had set up a couple of weeks earlier) and had no idea of what was coming. They didn't appear at all stressed; in fact, to them, it was just a normal morning. It was a shock for me at first but, like everything in life, you get used to it.

The animals are killed humanely with a bolt gun. They are then bled, gutted and skinned – the slaughterman will take away the waste. I usually hang the carcass for the relevant amount of time (the slaughterman can advise you on this), with a few bunches of mint covered in muslin cloth to deter flies. I then have the slaughterman come back at a later date and butcher the carcass for me.

It is possible to slaughter your livestock yourself. I personally wouldn't be able to do it, and you must be absolutely confident in what you are doing in order to avoid causing and pain or distress. Any slaughter has to be carried out humanely – visit the Food Standards Agency website for the UK guidelines on humane slaughter (see Resources, page 220).

Home slaughter is legal but is not promoted, and the law says you must not sell or give away any of the meat – it is only for your own consumption. Make sure you have enough freezer space to store everything. My appreciation for the food my animals give me is huge and I waste very little.

Abattoir

It is more common for smallholders to book their animals into an abattoir for slaughter. There are lots of regulations on slaughter and these vary depending on where you live (see Resources, page 220).

I think using a smaller abattoir is much better if there is one nearby. Ask around and do some research to find the best abattoir for your animals. It is best to book your abattoir well in advance to be sure of getting your preferred date.

Speak to the abattoir ahead of the slaughter and find out what you can expect on the day. You should also ask them what paperwork is needed and when they will need to receive it (some abattoirs prefer to receive paperwork in advance, others will accept it on the day). You will need to make sure that your animals have the appropriate ear tags/ID/slap marks beforehand – again, the abattoir can advise you on this.

You need to arrange the appropriate transport for your animals (see page 204) and oversee them while they are travelling to keep them calm. They are your responsibility right up until dispatch. Some smallholders prefer to drop their animals off and leave before the actual slaughter, whilst others prefer to wait with their animals – this is your choice.

Some abattoirs will process and butcher the meat for you, or send it to a butcher to be prepared, then send it on to you ready for consumption. If your meat has been slaughtered in an abattoir, it is legal for you to feed/give it to people outside your household, unlike with a home slaughter. Most smallholders probably won't produce enough meat to sell on, but it is legal to do so if it has been slaughtered at an abattoir and butchered there or by an approved butcher. However, as with anything, there are rules! For up-to-date information, the FSA website is great. Research what cuts of meat you want before you go – the abattoir/butcher will advise you, but having an idea of what the options are will help. When I had my first animal butchered, I had no idea, and although we got there in the end I did feel pretty silly! Remember, the first time you do anything in life it's scary, but the more you do it the easier it becomes.

RIGHT: As well as being friendly and easy to handle, Dexters produce lovely meat.

 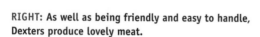

6

BEEKEEPING

Beekeeping is making a comeback and is popular in both rural and urban settings. Some people keep bees to harvest their honey, some to help pollination within their smallholding, while some just want to help with bee conservation. Bee numbers are dwindling rapidly as their habitats are disturbed and changed. Agricultural farming of single crops over vast areas is no good for bees, as they require variety. Pesticides are also harmful – in China, due to excessive use of pesticides and the lack of a natural habitat, the bee population has been eradicated. Farmers are having to hand-pollinate their crops with pots of pollen and paintbrushes – total madness!

Pollination is necessary for plants to reproduce. When the bees collect pollen and nectar they fertilise the flowers or blossom as they go. It's such a simple process when done by a bee as nature intended. Bee numbers are stable at the moment, but they still need our help, so planting bee-friendly plants or keeping your own hive is an excellent idea.

Bees are fascinating. Watching them busily flying in and out of their hive on a sunny evening can be rather relaxing and is a good way to clear your head of day-to-day niggles. When you begin to understand the real importance of this tiny insect, it makes you realise how fragile our ecosystem is. Before you rush

off to buy any beekeeping equipment, I would recommend that you do a beekeeping course. There is so much to learn and you really need to have knowledge for your venture to be a success. If you are in the UK, the British Beekeepers Association has a really good website (www.bbka.org.uk) where you can find groups local to you. You could also go along to a local agricultural show, find the beekeeping tent and have a talk to some dedicated beekeepers. There are courses and often mentoring schemes where an experienced beekeeper will team up with you and help you while you set up and gain confidence. Do as much research as you can before getting started. You should also consult with any nearby neighbours before setting up a hive.

There are about 25,000 known species of bees in the world.

I'm not a huge fan of wasps – in fact, I am one of those people who will scream and shout when pestered by them – and for a very long time, this put me off bees. However, I now see that having a friendly colony of bees that you understand and treat calmly and well can be a true asset to any smallholding. However, before proceeding, you should consider carefully whether you or your family are severely allergic to bee stings!

how a colony works

Colonies work as a unit where all the bees are dependent on each other.

The queen controls the hive; she excretes a pheromone that triggers a social response within her colony and she lays all the eggs.

Worker bees are the 'brains' of the hive and are split into three groups:

- Guard bees, who guard the entrance and watch all visitors to the hive; they identify intruders by smell and will attack and drive them away.
- House bees, who look after the young and keep the hive clean.
- Forager bees, who are busy every day collecting pollen and nectar, flying over 3km just to forage.

Drone bees are male honeybees. I call them 'the big boys' as they are considerably bigger than other bees. They do little around the hive, spending most of the day lazing around, helping themselves to the nectar stores – they don't even clean or help out with the kids! The downside to this easy lifestyle is that they

THE SMALLHOLDER'S HANDBOOK

do not live long – they die after mating and when the going gets tough in the winter, they are the first to be pushed out of the colony! Drones do not sting.

You need to be able to understand your colony to pre-empt and deal with swarming. This happens when a new queen is born. The old queen will fly away with up to 60 per cent of the worker bees (this is a swarm), leaving behind a new virgin queen and workers. Swarming is the natural way that honeybees reproduce colonies, so from one colony, two are born! A queen can only reproduce with a sufficient-sized colony. An individual queen, drone or worker will not survive for long.

You need to learn the signs of imminent swarming and understand their life cycle to be able to do these amazing insects justice. The appearance of queen cells (see page 215) is the first sign of swarming. Look out for changes in behaviour in the worker bees – do they appear less active? This could mean they are conserving their energy and getting themselves ready to build the new nest. The queen will also be starved so that she slims down, enabling her to fly.

setting up a hive

As I have already mentioned, the very first thing to do is to book yourself onto a good beekeeping course – you can't start keeping bees without one! You need knowledge and confidence to handle them correctly and provide a good environment. After that, you can start gathering the correct equipment.

You will need:
• **a bee suit** – This can be new or second-hand. Full suits are best, but for speed and coolness in hot weather experienced beekeepers often use bee jackets. Traditionally, bee suits are white or cream but now you can purchase them in different colours; the colour has no effect on the bees or their performance.

ABOVE: A smoker is a crucial piece of beekeeping equipment.

• **gloves** – I favour supple, long, leather gloves, but they can be clumsy to work in and some say they even attract bees. Other people favour rubber washing-up gloves. Whatever you choose, the most important thing is to make sure they fit you and to wash them regularly.

• **Wellington boots** – No one wants bees up their trouser legs!

• **a smoker** – Usually a metal canister, this consists of a little firepot in which to burn fuel, bellows, and a nozzle which can be used to direct the smoke. It is essential to calm/distract the bees when you need to examine the hive. You need to 'smoke' the hive before you open it. Normally, when a hive is opened the guard bees release a pheromone alerting their fellow guards to attack the intruder. However, if you smoke the hive first, the pheromones are masked and they will not attack.

The smoke also has the added effect of making the bees think the hive is on fire, so they instinctively gorge themselves on the honey, distracting them from you. You can use twigs and straw as fuel for the smoker, but cocoa shell is great as it burns for longer and emits a cooler smoke.

- **a hive tool** – This will help you open up the hive and manipulate the frames as they will be rather sticky. Hive tools are often brightly coloured, so you can locate them easily if dropped.

- **a bee brush** – This is used to gently brush bees out of the way when you are closing the hive.

- **honey extractors** –These are mechanical devices that are used to remove honey from the honeycomb. They are expensive to buy, but can be hired from some beekeeping clubs. Look online, as there is lots of information on how to make your own. See page 216 for how to extract honey without one.

But most importantly of all, you will have to purchase a hive.

A lot of people love the traditional 'WBC' hives, named after their inventor William Broughton Carr. Although lovely to look at, they are rather impractical to use as you need to remove the outer part of the structure in order to gain access to examine the hive.

The National Hive is the most commonly chosen hive – a basic box shape, it is not as pretty, but is functional and easy to use.

The Beehaus is a very modern, plastic beehive, which is becoming very popular as it is easy to clean and move and comes complete with everything you need to start. I love it; it is so easy to use and looks good, too.

The best tip I can give you when choosing a hive is to take advice from your local club, who will be able to tell you what neighbouring beekeepers have been successful with.

Although the different types of hive can vary quite a lot, the basic components are the same, from the top down:

Roof with crown board – This keeps the hive dry and allows ventilation.

Super with vertical hanging frames – This is where the bees store their surplus honey, and where you can collect it from.

ABOVE, FROM LEFT: A smoker ready to be used; smoking the hive (I would strongly advise wearing gloves and a full bee suit, but Matt is a real Devon boy and extremely confident around his bees!); the bees are calm after the smoking.

Queen excluder – This is an entranceway to the super that allows the worker bees through but not the queen or drones. Using a queen excluder prevents eggs being laid in the super, which is where you want to collect your honey.

Brood chamber with vertical hanging board – This is where the bees reproduce.

Floor and entrance – The bottom layer of the hive, and also where the bees will go in and out.

Where you position your hives is called an apiary or beeyard. It should be established away from people; you do not want it by your back door, for obvious reasons, so an unused spot at the end of your garden is ideal. If placing it in a field, don't site it right next to any animals. Bees can irritate some animals, added to which if any livestock decide to have a scratch on the hive it may well fall over, which will anger the bees – I wouldn't want to see that! Pigs can sniff honey out, and you don't want to come back to a contented, gorged pig and a flattened hive!

Ideally, aim to place your hive in a south- or southeast-facing position so the bees are woken early by the sun and encouraged out of the hive. I wish it were that easy with teenage boys! Placing the hive near a hedge or tree is advantageous, as this encourages the bees to take a higher flight path, rather than going straight into the neighbour's garden. They should go straight up and over and, once up, bees tend to keep to their flight path (unless blown down by the wind!), so this will encourage them to go further before they descend. Hedges and trees also offer protection from the wind and provide shade in hot weather.

If no shade is available it may be necessary to provide some, as hives in direct sunlight can become extremely hot.

TOP RIGHT: **The commonly used National Hive.**
RIGHT: **My new Beehaus hive is easy to clean and use.**

getting a colony

When setting up a colony, you need to purchase a healthy, even-tempered 'nucleus', which is a group of bees in all stages of development. It should include a laying queen and enough worker bees to cover three to five combs (a comb is where the bees store their honey and larvae). Buying from a local reputable breeder is advisable, and it is recommended that you buy bees that have been bred locally or at least within your country. Collecting an unwanted swarm requires skill, so is not advisable for a beginner; the bees could be diseased or rather bad-tempered.

Buying your colony from a local breeder means the bees will be used to the local area and a knowledgeable breeder will not be far away if help is needed.

Most people go for one hive, but I think two is a better option: if one colony dies – this does sometimes happen, even if you are doing everything right – you will have none left. Also, if you have two hives, you can compare different techniques to see which work better for you.

Types of bees

Western Honey Bee or European Honey Bee – Native to Europe, Asia and Africa, these bees produce plenty of honey. They vary in colour; some are black or brown intermixed with yellow.

German Honey Bee – Dark in colour, these bees are known for being rather defensive, which makes keeping them tricky. They are rare as they are often affected by diseases.

Carniolan Bee – Popular in the US due to their docile nature, they are great builders of wax combs that can be used for candle making, soaps and cosmetics.

The Buckfast Bee – Created by a monk from Buckfast Abbey, these bees are hardy and produce good honey. They are moderately defensive.

Russian Bee – One of the newest bee stocks in the US, Russian Bees are quite resistant to the varroa mite (see page 217). They overwinter well, produce a good amount of honey and are easy to manage.

Italian Bee – Also favoured in the US, these are excellent honey producers and easy to work with. They are a gorgeous lemon colour.

caring for your bees

You need to inspect your hives weekly to check on the bees' health and keep an eye on queen cells – these are the cells where queen eggs are laid. If a queen egg is present, the cell will be built into a queen cup. These are larger than the cells of the normal brood comb and rise vertically above the others. If you spot a queen cell, this is a warning that the colony will swarm. As with anything, the more you carry out your checks, the easier it will become as you will learn what to look out for. Your weekly inspections should involve checking that the queen is present by either spotting her or checking for evidence of her by looking for freshly laid eggs. Check your frames; look at the sealed honey and brood. A sealed brood is usually brown whereas sealed honeycomb is lighter in colour, white or yellow. Check that the bees appear healthy and are increasing in number, and check that you have enough frames in the hive to cater for the number of bees – you may be able to add more if they are needed. Observe their behaviour – as you get to know them, you will be quick to spot any signs of abnormality.

Checking your hive should take no longer than half an hour once you get the hang of it.

LEFT: Matt inspecting his hive. It is advisable to wear gloves and a bee suit – Matt spends so much time with his bees they probably think he's part of the colony, but I'd still cover up more than he does!

extracting honey without an extractor

Place the honeycomb in a large, clean bucket. Remove it from the frame and break the honeycomb into as many pieces as you can – you can do this by hand, it's just difficult resisting the urge to lick your fingers! Using a large masher, crush the honeycomb into a mush; there should be no lumps that you could pick up by hand. Next, you need to strain the mixture. Place a straining bag or some muslin over the top of another clean bucket and secure it around the edge. Be prepared for things to get very messy at this stage! Carefully pour the mixture onto the cloth, so it can strain through into the bucket. This is a very slow process; sometimes you will need to scrape some of the mashed comb out into the strainer. When the honey is strained, you can transfer it to sterilised jars and admire your work.

collecting the honey

Bees take nectar (carbohydrate) and pollen (protein) and convert it into honey. What they do not use immediately is stored as winter food for when nectar is not available. When you see that the honeycombs are sealed with a wax capping, it signals harvest time. You need to remove the wax cap and then the honey, which is a very sticky job. It is almost impossible to resist the temptation to have a taste. I never take all the honey, as I prefer to leave some for the bees.

There are many ways to make this process easier, but it can be done with a warm knife and a muslin square. Once you have removed the cap from the honeycomb, squeeze the comb and collect the honey in jars. Using a centrifugal honey extractor is easiest. It spins so that most of the honey is expelled using centrifugal force. You can also eat the honey straight from the comb, which my children love. Any honey left on the frames after extraction can be left out for the bees to re-harvest. Do this early morning or late evening and away from your back door, as bees can be rather excited after such a find.

feeding

Having removed some of the honey for yourself, you need to replace it. It is common practice to do this by giving them a feed of sugar syrup in the autumn. Mix 1kg sugar with 0.5 litres of boiling water and allow to cool. Once this is done, you can place it in a feeder above the brood box. Never put syrup in open containers, as you will end up with lots of dead bees that have fallen in and drowned, so purchase a special feeder. As it has no smell, a very small amount of syrup or honey can be dribbled to provide a trail to the sugar syrup. If you have to feed your bees during the winter, icing sugar is the best thing to use as the bees can eat it straightaway.

Bees may need feeding at different times; at the end of a very long winter, or after the spring flowers have finished but before the summer ones have started. This can vary from hive to hive, but as you get to know your bees, you will learn.

health

As with all animals, bees can suffer from diseases, even when you do everything right. There are many health problems bees encounter. Listed opposite are just a few problematic ones that seem to be prevalent in a lot of areas.

Foulbrood

There are two types of this condition. The American foulbrood, which is rare in the UK, is highly contagious with no treatment available. If suspected, you should contact the National Bee Unit (NBU, see below), and, if confirmed, the bees will be destroyed. You will need an experienced beekeeper to spot it – the cappings on the comb will appear sunken, moist and discoloured and when opened you will see diseased larvae and pupae. In the later stages, American foulbrood has a distinctive smell. European foulbrood is the most common form and spreads quickly but it can be treated. An indicator of European foulbrood is larvae being dead before they are sealed in their cell. Larvae often collapse, almost as if they had been melted, turning a yellowish colour and then drying up. This disease also has a very distinctive smell if the infection is severe. Again, the NBU should be contacted.

Mites

The most serious threat to bees is the varroa mite, which is present in nearly all UK hives. It is a bloodsucking mite the size of a pinhead and chestnut in colour. Chemicals are available to treat mites, but must be used with care.

Stress

Like us, bees can also be affected by stress so avoid over-management. It is very exciting when you get a new hive as you want to be hands-on, but you should avoid disturbing them too often. Once a week is fine. Moving hives can cause stress to bees, as can as the weather. Bees can cope with a little bit of stress but, when it is ongoing, it can and does kill colonies. When they are stressed, bees will exhibit erratic behaviour, appearing almost drunk, as it can affect their orientation and mobility skills. Persistent rain and winds can cause considerable stress; a few of my very experienced beekeeper friends lost all of their hives during one very wet period recently.

ABOVE: Removing the hanging board to check all is well in the hive.

For more information, in the UK you can consult the National Bee Unit (NBU – www.nationalbeeunit.com) or the Food and Environment Research Agency (Fera) (www.fera.co.uk). They provide apiary inspections, disease diagnosis and training. Beekeeping associations in many areas offer self-help schemes and advice, so contact your local group, bee inspector or Disease Liaison Co-ordinator for help and information.

resources

Guidelines and Legal
The organisations and information listed below relate to UK rules and regulations. If you are outside the UK, consult your own government's guidelines, as these may vary.

General
Animal & Plant Health Agency (APHA) – formerly AVLHA
www.gov.uk/government/organisations/animal-and-plant-health-agency
Postcode tool – http://avhla.defra.gov.uk/postcode/index.asp

Department for Environment, Food and Rural Affairs (DEFRA)
www.defra.gov.uk
03459335577

European Forum for Animal Welfare Councils
www.eurofawc.com

Food and Environment Research Agency (FERA)
www.fera.co.uk
01904462000

Rural Payments Agency (RPA)
www.gov.uk/government/organisations/rural-payments-agency
03456037777

Trading Standards
www.tradingstandards.gov.uk

Transport
www.gov.uk/farm-animal-welfare-during-transportation

World Organisation for Animal Health
www.oie.int

Slaughter
www.gov.uk/farm-animal-welfare-at-slaughter

Humane Slaughter Association
www.hsa.org.uk

Cows
British Cattle Movement Service (BCMS)
www.bcms.gov.uk
03450501234

Pigs
Electronic Pig Movement Service
www.eaml2.org.uk
08443358400

Sheep
British Wool Marketing Board
www.britishwool.org.uk

Bees
British Beekeeper's Association
www.bbka.org.uk
08718112282 or 08718112337

National Bee Unit (NBU)
www.nationalbeeunit.com
03003030094

Recommended Products & Suppliers
Below are just some of the products and suppliers I use in the day-to-day running of my smallholding. They are UK-based, but many of the products are available internationally.

Electric Fencing Direct
These guys are really great. Their products are fantastic and they are very knowledgeable – there is always someone available to help out.
www.electricfencing.co.uk
01620860058

Fancy Feed Company
Speciality feed that is great for poultry and waterfowl.
www.fancyfeedcompany.co.uk
01371850247

The Farmer's Friend
Suppliers of high-quality, well-priced outdoor clothes. Fantastic service and speedy delivery.
www.farmersfriend.co.uk
01392 277024

Gold Label Direct
Sunblock for animals and other health products.
www.goldlabeldirect.co.uk
07721411620

Omlet
As well as making great plastic chicken housing with runs,

Omlet are also the makers of the fantastic plastic Beehaus beehive.
www.omlet.co.uk
08454502056

Radmore & Tucker
The best place to get all your machinery and protective clothing. Great service from very knowledgeable people.
www.radmoretucker.co.uk
01392279429

Smallholder Range
A range of feed designed for free-ranging animals. Free from GM products.
www.smallholderfeed.co.uk
01362822902

Verm–X
Natural wormers and tonic for all smallholding animals. It works really well and is 100% organic. Available internationally.
www.verm–x.com
08708502313

Recommended Breeders
Breeders are often very localised, so I recommend you ask around in your local area to find the best breeders to approach for your needs. Those listed below are ones I can personally recommend.

Hollybush Farm
A unique place with an array of rarebreed livestock for smallholdings, including cows,

pigs, sheep, goats and poultry. Very friendly and helpful.
www.hollybushrarebreeds.co.uk
07584023078

Norsworthy Dairy Goats
These dairy goat farmers sell beautiful unpasteurised cheeses handmade with their goat's milk.
01363775326

Shilford Herd – Pedigree Dexter Cattle
Bernard Stamp raises great Dexters. He has bulls available for hire and sells semen from his top UK show bull.
01392833694
stamp.dexters@freeuk.com

Willmar Flock – Pedigree Suffolk Sheep
The best sheep every time, and an extremely helpful and knowledgeable shepherd.
01392832281

glossary

This is a short glossary to cover some of the less common terms that are used frequently in the book.

Boar
An adult male pig.

Candling
A method for viewing the developing chick inside an egg by shining a light on it (see page 71).

Chick crumb
Feed with high protein content design for very young chicks.

Crop/land rotation
The practice of dividing land into sections and varying what crops are grown on it, or which animals graze it, in order to allow the ground to recover (see pages 38–39).

CPH Number
County Parish Holding number (see page 50).

Diatomaceous earth
A soft rock that is found in white powder form. It is an effective insecticide and can be used to control mite and flea infestations.

Does
Female goats (also called nannies).

Farrowing
The birthing process for pigs.

Field Shelter
A structure used to provide animals with shelter in fields. Usually open on one side. See page 27.

Finisher's pellets
Readymade pellet feed, tailored to each species to provide them with the proteins and nutrients they need to make them ready for the table.

Five Freedoms
Crucial internationally recognised guidelines for caring for animals (see page 48).

Gilt
A young female pig that has never been pregnant.

Grower's/Rearer's pellets
Readymade pellet feed, tailored to each species to provide them with the nutrients they need as they grow.

Hurdles
Pieces of lightweight portable fencing (see page 24).

Keet
A young guinea fowl.

Layer's pellets
Readymade pellet feed, tailored to bird species to provide them with the nutrients they need to lay healthy eggs.

Mixed grit
A mixture of oyster shell (a source of calcium) and flint grit (which helps to grind food in the gizzard), given to birds to aid digestion.

Navel dip/spray
An iodine-based liquid that you dip or spray onto the navel after birth. It prevents infection entering via the unhealed navel – crucial, as infections can lead to fatal septicaemia.

Pasture
Any material grazed by livestock (see pages 44–45).

Pullet
A female chicken before she has laid her first egg (afterwards, she is a hen).

Sow
An adult female pig, usually one that has farrowed.

Unique herd/flock number
A unique number assigned by the Animal and Plant Health Agency (APHA) to help identify a herd or flock (see page 50).

Vent
A bird's bottom.

index

First published in Great Britain in 2015 by
Kyle Books, an imprint of Kyle Cathie Ltd
192–198 Vauxhall Bridge Road
London SW1V 1DX
general.enquiries@kylebooks.com
www.kylebooks.com

10 9 8 7 6 5 4 3 2 1

ISBN 978 0 85783 272 6

Text © 2015 Suzie Baldwin
Design © 2015 Kyle Books
Photographs © 2015 Rachel Warne*
*except pages 34–35 © shutterstock/Kononova Viktoriya; page 83 © shutterstock/
Amy McNabb; page 86 © shutterstock Elliotte Rusty Harold; page 92 ©
shutterstock/Kostrez; page 99 © istock photo/Danakia; page 138 © shutterstock/
poeticpenguin; page 155 left © shutterstock/Arina P Habich; page 155 right ©
shutterstock/Godrick; page 157 (both) © shutterstock/StockHouse; page 162 ©
shutterstock/Air Images

Suzie Baldwin is hereby identified as the author of this work
in accordance with Section 77 of the Copyright, Designs and
Patents Act 1988.

Editor: Tara O'Sullivan
Proofreader: Polly Boyd
Designer: Carl Hodson
Photographer: Rachel Warne
Production: Lisa Pinnell

A Cataloguing in Publication record for this title is available
from the British Library.

Colour reproduction by ALTA London
Printed and bound in China by C&C Joint Printing CO., (GUANGDONG) LTD.

Special thanks go to Luke Gates for being a very
special person x

To all the people that helped out with this book –
you know who you are – drinks are on me!

Thank you to Matt Baker, Bernard Stamp, Mary Carr,
Rob Holmes and Tom Mead for all their help with the
photo shoots.

Thank you to Tara, who has been so patient, and to
Rachel and Carl for making the book beautiful.

Lastly, thank you to my ever–suffering husband and
children, who have taken the plunge with me and
worked so bloody hard to make this smallholding
lark possible.

THE SMALLHOLDER'S HANDBOOK